"*City Impact* is not only prophetic but practical, an end-times tool to help us transform our cities. As we put this cutting-edge book into practice, we can change our neighborhoods and our nation."

Pat Robertson, founder and chairman, the Christian Broadcasting Network

"Daniel writes passionately from the heart, like no one else I have read. If you are up for a challenge, read these pages. You will fall in love with your city and with the Lord at a deeper level than you thought possible."

Steve Sjogren, founding pastor, Vineyard Community Church, Cincinnati

"Daniel Bernard serves as a key city leader on the front lines of effective ministry in a major city and as a regional associate of the cities team of the Mission America Coalition. His practical insights and encouragement will be of significant help to anyone who desires to minister effectively in a city."

Dr. Paul Cedar, chairman, Mission America Coalition

"Daniel Bernard is reaching his city for Christ, and *City Impact* reflects his experience and vision. I have witnessed firsthand his passion for the lost and zeal for the Gospel. *City Impact* is a practical, inspirational tool for today's Church."

Terry Teykl, president, Renewal Ministries

"What a wonderful title and significant addition to any pastor's library! Daniel Bernard reminds us that the Church is bigger than the building on the corner. He offers many practical ideas for building and growing the Church of the city."

Glenn Barth, national facilitator for cities, Mission America Coalition

"*City Impact* is a divine call for this appointed hour. The truth found in the pages of this book can transform your life, your church and your city. It is essential for the Body of Christ today. Read it, take it to heart and do it!"

Jodi Nelson, director of outreach, Operation Blessing International

"Revival without compassion for the lost and without transformation for our communities will leave us with nothing but great meetings again. If you are looking for the recipe for good meetings, this book won't help you. But if you are looking to bring presence evangelism into your city, this is the book for you."

Bishop Bart Pie

"There is a paradigm shift taking place in the Body of Christ—from pastoring a congregation to pastoring a community—and leading to transformation. Daniel Bernard gives us a practical guide to the how-to of transformation that gives ideas and strategies born through prayer and the direction of the Holy Spirit. Workplace believers will find helpful advice as to their role in this important movement."

Os Hillman, director, International Coalition of Workplace Ministries

"I am grateful for Daniel Bernard's contributions in making St. Petersburg one of the most livable cities in America. He is helping me structure a faith-based initiative for organizations to adopt neighborhoods and work in partnership to improve the lives of people throughout the community."

Rick Baker, mayor, St. Petersburg, Florida

"Daniel Bernard's *City Impact* sounds a reveille, calling the Church to rise up and move out into the streets of our cities. I recommend this book without reservation to those who seek to fulfill the Church's joy-filled mandate to minister to the hurting, the lost and the seeking."

David Cerullo, president, the Inspiration Networks

"Daniel has captured what could and can be if people move outside themselves and go for it. It is easy to get caught up in church, meetings and budgets and forget the call and desire of the Lord. Jesus is not only Lord of the Church but also Lord of the harvest."

Pastor Doug Roe, Dayton (Ohio) Vineyard

"God is using Daniel Bernard in these days to bring local churches together for the sole purpose of impacting entire cities for the Kingdom of heaven. The goal is citywide transformation as the true Church, the Body of Christ, unites. *City Impact* will give you the passion, philosophy and practical steps necessary to be part of this great movement in our generation."

Pastor Ed Russo, Victorious Life Church, Tampa

"Daniel Bernard is a full-time, veteran, frontline, battle-scarred city-reacher. Do you want to love your city to Jesus? If so, Daniel Bernard's book overflows with practical ideas that can help you."

M. Barnett "Barney" Field, executive director, El Paso for Jesus

"This is a dynamic book in a time when the Church needs to be interwoven throughout the entire community and filled with a passionate love for God and a compassionate love for all people. It points out that Christians will be most used by their Creator when they are working alongside Christians of all denominations."

Dr. James P. Gills, St. Luke's Cataract & Eye Institute, Palm Harbor, Fla.

CITY IMPACT

How to Unify, Empower
and Mobilize God's People to
Transform Their Communities

DANIEL BERNARD

Chosen
Grand Rapids, Michigan

Published by Chosen Books
A division of Baker Publishing Group
P.O. Box 6287, Grand Rapids, MI 49516-6287
www.chosenbooks.com

Printed in the United States of America

Library of Congress Cataloging-in-Publication Data
Bernard, Daniel, 1956–
    City impact : how to unify, empower and mobilize God's people to
    transform their communities / Daniel Bernard.
        p.   cm.
    Includes bibliographical references.
    ISBN 0-8007-9376-5 (pbk.)
    1. City churches. I. Title.
BV37.B47 2004
253'.091732—dc22   2004009758

Contents

Preface

There is a whole lot of talk about unity among believers and the Body of Christ coming together. Everyone seems to see the problem but there are not many who seem to have a viable, sensible and workable solution to the problem of disunity and divisiveness among believers. If you are like me, you have read the same Scriptures over and over again about how the Body is one Body and the Church is one Church. I have searched and searched the Scriptures for a revelation that would challenge me to be more than a part of the problem but to become a part of the solution. I believe that I have found such a treatise and revelation in Daniel Bernard's new book.

You will read stirring current-day stories of how the obedience of common Christians can impact many. Daniel Bernard makes truth application that is both compelling and convicting. Daniel captures the heart of our God for His big "C" Church in the cities in which we abide. The keys given in this book can change not just a community but also the entire world if we can lay aside our own pettiness, personal lack and agendas and think large and think *one*. Unity, repentance and love are the marks of the Church of

Jesus Christ. This book reminds us of the need of all three to see the glory of God in these last days. God raised up Ehud, "Union," to turn a city around. But unity must be maintained. I have been challenged to maintain the unity of the Spirit in my community and not give up the prayer of our Lord, "Father, make them one." When you read this book, you will have some questions to answer and some work to do.

Unity takes effort. Unity takes sacrifice. Unity takes self-lessness. You can have no hidden agendas or ulterior motives if you expect to see what the apostles and the early Church experienced in their day. They believed and preached that there was one Lord, one faith and one baptism. The Bible teaches us that the Body is one Body. Have you gotten the revelation of how unity can be accomplished and how God can be glorified through our relationships with each other? If you have not gotten it right yet, this book can help you. If you have applied yourself to this task, then this book can only enhance what you already know and are applying to help transform your church and community as it relates to the Body of Christ coming together. Read it and do it and let us be the gift to our communities God has intended us to be.

Bishop Vaughn McLaughlin
The Potter's House Christian Fellowship
Jacksonville, Fla.

Foreword

Disunity is the single greatest threat to the Body of Christ. Read that sentence again.

Now read it again.

I know you have probably heard church leaders speak on this subject a thousand times. It is almost banal to mention it. Unity is a common theme because disunity is a common problem. Often it feels as though the best thing to do is just accept disunity as part of Christianity and go about our business as best we can.

But that is not an option. As long as churches are not working together, then the big-C Church (as Daniel Bernard calls it) will never really be the Church at all. So read that sentence again and again. Let its truth sink in. Let it motivate you to pray and to fight for unity. Because, as you will see throughout the book you are about to read, when churches discover how to defeat disunity and come together for the cause of Christ (and they sometimes do—they really do!), the world gets turned on its head. People come to life. God's Kingdom comes in a powerful way, and communities are transformed for good.

This, in a nutshell, is what Daniel Bernard believes, and it is what motivates the work he does every day. Daniel has a vision that is simple yet bold. If implemented, it can revolutionize whole cities—one sermon, one outreach, one conversation, one relationship, one person at a time.

Daniel begins this book by suggesting that the Church is God's gift to your city. Unfortunately, because we do not always do a good job of being that gift, many of our cities are like disappointed little boys on Christmas morning openings boxes of broken toys with missing parts and garbled instruction manuals. If the Church is a gift, then it has to be complete, presentable and ready to serve. If the Church is a gift, then it has to be in working order. If the Church is a gift, then it has to do what it was made to do.

As president of the National Association of Evangelicals, I have been traveling around a lot lately to a wide variety of parts of the Body of Christ. Do you know what I have found? No matter how striking our differences seem, we all really do want the same thing. From by-the-book Presbyterians to holy-rolling Pentecostals, at the end of the day all God's people just want to love Him, serve Him and do what He commands—love one another and love our neighbors as ourselves. That's it. Everyone from Missoula to Washington, D.C., wants the same thing, and they are all raring to go get it.

I believe the principles in this book will help them along the way. They will help us all realize the vision of unity. If disunity is the single greatest threat to the Body of Christ, then unity is the single greatest threat to the plan of the devil. So let's come together, get to work and learn how to be the gift that God wants us all to be.

Ted Haggard, president,
National Association of Evangelicals

I

God's Gift to Your City

What is God's gift to your city? Is it the new industry that has just decided to build its plant in your community? Is it the new mayor who just got elected? Is it new federal money to build better highways, schools and other public facilities?

These and other such things are certainly material blessings that we, as Christians, know ultimately come from God, because all good things come from above. God's greatest gift to our communities, however, is the Church, the Body of His Son. And it has been since its genesis on the Day of Pentecost. We may have not looked like it or acted like it, but the Church is God's gift to our cities. God wants cities to be places where systems are developed to benefit people. In other words, cities were created for the well-being of people in that society or community.

In Genesis 10, we find that Nimrod was a "mighty one" who built cities. But these cities were not serving their intended purpose. That is why the people of Babylon were

11

scattered. In Genesis 12, God sought a man and, through him, a people that He could bless to be a blessing to all nations. The Church, being the seed of Abraham, is now that people. One job of this people is to ensure that cities carry out their purpose—to create well-being for those who dwell there. You will recall that God destroyed the cities of Sodom and Gomorrah because they were well off but failed to tend to the welfare of their people.

Another biblical example of God's intentions for cities is found in the story of Jonah. God reprimanded Jonah for his lack of compassion for the city of Nineveh:

> "Should I not have compassion on Nineveh, the great city in which there are more than 120,000 persons who do not know the difference between their right and left hand, as well as many animals?"
>
> Jonah 4:11

God brought about revival and repentance in that pagan city, which produced a people who would follow Him and His purposes. When God said He felt compassion for the thousands there who did not know their right hand from their left, He was referring to innocent children who would suffer along with the city's rebellious adults. By mentioning animals, God showed the breadth of His compassion and His concern for the economic development of the city, which was related to them. He was saying, "I have concern for the future well-being of this city and the people who live in it and so should you as one of My servants."

As God's gift to a city, we are the ones who look out for the welfare of God's creation in a city. You will read in the next chapter how Jesus, Himself, wanted to embrace Jerusalem. He wanted the city to know His providence, protection and provision. The welfare of people in Jerusalem and other cities was His concern. The ultimate source of well-being for people in any city, of course, is to come under the gentle rule of their Savior and King, Jesus.

For us to become God's gift to our city, we must first be the big "C" Church. I will share why I believe we have not been that gift and how we can be that gift when we serve together. We will also look at places where the Church is manifesting itself as the gift. The following story, from Steve Sjogren's book *The Perfectly Imperfect Church*, is one example of how we can be the gift God intended as we become the big "C" Church:

> As the woman worked in her garden, her not-yet-Christian neighbor approached her. He asked, "Are you a member of the big church?"
>
> Earlier that day the woman had been a part of a citywide event in her hometown of Abbotsford, British Columbia, near Vancouver in western Canada. Christians in this city of about one hundred thousand began an experiment a couple of years ago. They banded together to serve their city in large-scale, creative, and profound ways. I have been privileged to be a part of training those doing outreach. It is always exciting to train motivated people.
>
> At the last event they held, which they dubbed Love Abbotsford, some fourteen hundred people from thirty local churches came out for various serving projects around the city. Everyone wore a white T-shirt with a large heart on it and handed out cards to explain the projects. The cards didn't promote individual churches but the big "C" church in the city. The cards named the Love Abbotsford event and referred people to a shared website that explained the entire project. The day went smoothly. Many thousands of people were touched, and the participants came back enthused.
>
> Now back to the woman working in her garden that afternoon. Her not-yet-Christian neighbor stopped by and asked, "Say, I was in town today and saw all the folks with T-shirts. Are you a part of the big church with the T-shirts?"
>
> She thought for a second about her church, which had several hundred people. "Well, my church is pretty big."

The neighbor said, "No, the *really* big church, the one with the hundreds of people who were out on the town today—that church." She got it. Her heart was touched, she teared up, and she said, "Yes, in fact, I am a part of the big church!"

God is busy building the big church these days. If we are going to be a Perfectly Imperfect Church, we need to be larger than a single church. God has much for us to accomplish. We'll reach our potential only as we team up with the larger church.[1]

Sjogren follows this story with some penetrating questions:

What if . . . we realized the truth that we can't reach our city by ourselves, even if our church is large and well-equipped? We need an army made up of all the churches in our city.

What if . . . we were willing to cooperate with other churches, even churches that don't necessarily hold all the same traditions and opinions that we do?

What if . . . we prayed each weekend that God would bless the churches of the city first before He blessed our church—and we meant it?

What if . . . we really got along?

What if . . . we looked out for one another in the church scene? If one church gets a good name, we will all benefit from it; if one church gets a bad name, we will all suffer for it. It only makes sense that we begin to take seriously the reputation of the entire church in the city.

What if . . . God doesn't see us as being in different churches? What if God just sees those people who don't belong to His church? It doesn't make sense to compete with other churches. Rather we need to seek the people who are not connected with any church. There are thousands of those folks near you.

What if . . . we came alongside other people's dreams and blessed those dreams?

What if . . . we saw our well-being interwoven with the well-being of other churches in the city?[2]

When the "what ifs" become a reality, you get a city that is being embraced by Jesus. You get the big "C" Church becoming God's gift to that city. You get *city impact*!

Jesus Said You Would Have Impact

In Matthew 5:14–16, Jesus says we are the light of the world and that we will shine in such a way that others will see our good works and praise our Father in heaven. In John 14:12, Jesus says that our works will have even greater impact than His own. In other words, we are to have an impact on the whole world. And the majority of the world's population lives in cities. So to fulfill the Great Commission, we must have *city impact*. In Acts 1:8, Jesus says that the first-century disciples would have impact when the Holy Spirit came upon them. Their impact would begin in their own backyards and extend to the ends of the earth. How do we have city impact? The answer is in the question. The key is that *we do* it. The early Church had city and world impact because the people were of one accord (see Acts 4:32).

> **To fulfill the Great Commission, we must have *city impact*.**

As a missionary to Nigeria, I took nine young men and discipled them. One concept I tried to impart to them was how their area of service was helping build God's Kingdom in West Africa.

When I entered our building, I would often encounter the men doing their daily chores. One would be cleaning in

15

the kitchen, another sweeping the rooms. "What are you doing?" I would ask.

"We are sweeping (or cleaning)," would be the usual reply, at least at first.

I would shake my head. "No. You're not just sweeping or doing dishes," I would say. "Your service is building Christ in you so that you can impart the Kingdom of God in West Africa."

As members of God's Church serve Him faithfully, they help build the Kingdom of God. It took several times, but they eventually grasped the idea. If we are going to have the impact Christ said we would, we will need to understand that what we do does not just build our program or congregation but also the Kingdom of God in our city.

> **It is obedience in smaller areas of service that makes the larger impact possible.**

As you read this book you are going to learn about a lot of big-picture Kingdom-building city-reaching activities. As you read these accounts, be aware that none of them could have taken place without individuals who understood that their obedience in a smaller area of service made the larger impact possible. The following fictional story illustrates my point:

A doctor in a small French village was about to retire. He had given of himself for many years, serving the people. They could not afford to pay him much, but he cared for them as he was able. As the day of his retirement approached the people wanted to make an expression of their gratitude and affection. Someone proposed that since they had so little money to give, each family would bring wine from its own cellar, according to their ability, and pour it into a large barrel in the village square. The barrel of wine would then be given to the doctor as an expression of their gratitude.

The evening came and the barrel of wine was taken to the doctor's home and presented with all the inevitable speeches of endearment. When the presentation ended, the people drifted home, leaving the doctor alone in the glow of their love. After a while, he went to the barrel and drew off a bit of wine and sat down by the fire to enjoy it. The first sip was a shock. It tasted like water. He sipped again. It *was* water. He went back to the barrel and drew off more, thinking there must be some mistake. But no, the barrel was filled with water. The truth dawned. Each person in the village had reasoned: "My contribution of wine won't be missed. Others will take care of it. The little water I substitute will not be noticed." It is a tragic story. But it shows the way many people respond to stewardship. God's work goes on when we each contribute. We have the sad power to turn the wine of vision into the water of dilution—if we neglect to do our part.[3]

"Let someone else do it" or "My best won't make a difference" are ideas we cannot afford in these last days. Our power has been diluted because churchgoers in America have too often become spectators, throwing money at ministries and pastors to do the work, without becoming personally involved. With this philosophy, we void our authority and dilute our influence in our cities.

My message to you is that we can have an impact on whole communities. But know that *you* play a vital role in seeing that His will comes about in your city. I hope that through the ideas and real-life examples in this book, you will come to know your part, if you do not already. One by one, as we say yes to God's plan to reach our communities, we will be the gift God intended us to be. The church that becomes God's gift to its city affects its community. Just imagine for a minute what would happen if the congregations came together as the big "C" Church in your community. Ask God how you can contribute. You cannot have God-sized impact without God embracing the Church in your city. Be encouraged. Jesus wants to embrace your city.

2

Jesus Wants to Embrace Your City

George Otis Jr., Christian author and president of the Sentinel Group, put together the popular documentary videos called *Transformations* that show what happens when churches become the big "C" Church in a city. These productions also detail the results when the "what ifs" of Steve Sjogren become "what is" or reality.

The results are impressive. In Cali, Colombia, the drug cartels are being brought down and fifty thousand believers filled a stadium to praise Jesus. In Alamonga, Guatemala, the jails have been closed—because there is no crime. The people there are prospering as never before because the land is yielding fruit and vegetables in gargantuan size. Scientists cannot explain the phenomenon. It can only be explained through 2 Chronicles 7:14, where God promises He will heal our land if His people, called by His name, will "humble themselves and pray and seek My face and turn from their wicked ways." In this chapter, I will show how Jesus sought to embrace the city of Jerusalem but could not. Jesus wants to embrace cities today. Our response to Him will make the difference.

"Would" or "Would Not" Cities

We read in Luke 13:34 how Jesus sought to embrace Jerusalem:

> "O Jerusalem, Jerusalem, the city that kills the prophets and stones those sent to her! How often I wanted to gather your children together, just as a hen gathers her brood under her wings, and you would not have it!"

Jesus was saying to Jerusalem, "I wanted to embrace you. I wanted you to know My protection, provision and providence, but you *would not*." They refused. They rejected the Bridegroom's embrace.

In these last days the arms of our Savior are extended once again to cities throughout the earth. The Bridegroom, Jesus, is calling His Bride in each community to receive Him. Jesus is addressing God's people in Luke 13, especially their leaders. And today, just as in Christ's day, there will be "would" and "would not" cities. We, His Church, determine whether people in our cities will or will not experience the full embrace of Christ. Notice Luke 13:35:

It is the Church that determines whether or not our cities experience Christ's embrace.

> "Behold, your house is left to you desolate; and I say to you, you shall not see Me until the time comes when you say, 'Blessed is He who comes in the name of the Lord!'"

In other words, Jesus is saying, "Because you have rejected My embrace, your house will be left desolate. Just to prove that what I am saying is true, you will not see Me until the time when you say, 'Blessed is He who comes in the name of the Lord.'" This prophecy was fulfilled when Jesus made what is called His triumphal entry into Jerusalem in the final week before He was crucified. In Luke 19:37–41, we find the fulfillment of Christ's words:

> As soon as He was approaching, near the descent of the Mount of Olives, the whole crowd of the disciples began to praise God joyfully with a loud voice for all the miracles which they had seen, shouting: "Blessed is the King who comes in the name of the Lord; Peace in heaven and glory in the highest!" Some of the Pharisees in the crowd said to Him, "Teacher, rebuke Your disciples." But Jesus answered, "I tell you, if these become silent, the stones will cry out!" When He approached Jerusalem, He saw the city and wept over it.

It seems that the Pharisees whom Jesus addressed in Luke 13 are in the crowd, those with whom Jesus shared that supernatural word of knowledge from the Father. Since the Pharisees experience here the fulfillment of the prophecy, they cannot deny it. Our merciful Father was giving them one final opportunity to accept Jesus as their Messiah. Through this supernatural display, Jesus was one last time extending His loving arms to these religious people to accept Him. What was their response? "Teacher, rebuke Your disciples." Thus their final opportunity passes.

When Jesus approaches and sees the city, He weeps over it. Then anguish turns into righteous anger as Jesus explicitly foretells Jerusalem's fate. Jesus has predicted in Luke 13:35 that their house will be left desolate. Now as we read Luke 19:41–44, we see the extent of the desolation they will experience:

> When He approached Jerusalem, He saw the city and wept over it, saying, "If you had known in this day, even you, the

21

things which make for peace! But now they have been hidden from your eyes. For the days will come upon you when your enemies will throw up a barricade against you, and surround you and hem you in on every side, and they will level you to the ground and your children within you, and they will not leave in you one stone upon another, because you did not recognize the time of your visitation."

Mk. 6.1-6

In A.D. 70, history tells us, Jerusalem was destroyed and not one stone was left laid upon another. In the words above, Jesus tells us why Jerusalem was destroyed: "Because you did not recognize [perceive or understand] the time of your visitation." Jesus once again is reaching out to embrace the communities of the world. Do you perceive it?

Desolation, Visitation or Habitation?

I am sure you, like me, do not want anything like the desolation of Jerusalem to happen in your community! We must then ask the question: Do we want to go beyond visitation to habitation? We, as the Church, have often been satisfied with a visitation from God. By visitation I mean a season where the presence of God is manifested and at work among His people and in the community. The good fruit of souls being saved, backsliders returning to God, as well as unity and service being evident in the community are signs of a visitation of God. Often it lasts for the length of the revival or crusade. At times we have seen special outpourings, such as at the Asbury or Brownsville revivals, both genuine visitations of the Spirit of God.

> **Do we want a visit from God—or His habitation among us?**

In October 1998 we, the Church in Tampa Bay, hosted a Billy Graham Crusade. About seventy thousand people attended each night and there were more than twenty thousand

22

decisions made for Christ. It was a great visitation for that one week. A previous Billy Graham Crusade was held back in 1979. It, too, was a wonderful experience. But, as great as the crusades are, I do not want to wait for another twenty years for a visitation when we can have habitation.

Habitation is not short term but long term. It is where whole communities are transformed for generations. But we must prepare. The transformations being realized in Cali, Colombia, and Alamonga, Guatemala, have taken years to come about.

I believe Jesus, the God Man, is passing by. Do you perceive it? Will you do what it takes to see not just a visitation but also a habitation of the Son of God in your city?

We learn a vital lesson about ensuring this habitation from a woman in biblical history who understood the importance of creating a place for a man of God. The chapters that follow will describe how to create an atmosphere for habitation and how to make your city irresistible to Jesus. Let's review the story told in 2 Kings of this remarkable woman.

She is a Shunammite, and she is someone with perception who takes action that leads to blessing. Elisha often passes by Shunem and when he does, she persuades him to stop and rest.

> She said to her husband, "Behold now, I perceive that this is a holy man of God passing by us continually. Please, let us make a little walled upper chamber and let us set a bed for him there, and a table and a chair and a lampstand; and it shall be, when he comes to us, that he can turn in there." One day he came there and turned in to the upper chamber and rested.
>
> 2 Kings 4:9–11

The Shunammite woman recognizes that a man of God is in their midst. She is not satisfied with a visitation. She desires habitation on the part of the man of God. She wants him to reside comfortably in her home and even makes it difficult to leave such an atmosphere.

Elisha is overwhelmed with this kindness and asks, "What can I do for you?" (verse 13). She has only one real need and the servant Gehazi observes it, "Truly she has no son and her husband is old" (verse 14). Elisha prophesies that she will bear a son, and the following year the prophecy comes to pass.

The woman is much like the Church in the cities of America. We have no real need except one: We need a move of God to be birthed in our cities. Just as the Shunammite woman was barren, so are the majority of our cities. They are barren for a genuine move of God. Most have never experienced the manifest presence of God. In other cities, a move of God's Spirit occurred several generations ago and nothing has taken place since. The Shunammite woman knows material prosperity; what she really needs is for God to do a supernatural work and make her barren womb fruitful so she can give birth to a son. In the same way, the prosperous Church in the United States needs God to birth a move of His Spirit into our barren cities.

> **When our cry is for a move of God in our cities, He will hear and act.**

Notice that the woman moves Elisha. He feels he has to do something for her. Imagine that, Church. We, like the Shunammite woman, can so move Jesus that He will say, "I must do something for the Church in that city." I believe we can create a habitation for Jesus that will be irresistible. The Church in a city that has unity, love, desperate prayer and humility is a place that will become irresistible to Him. When Jesus sees these qualities in our cities He will ask, like Elisha, "What can I do for you?" Our reply is, "We do not need anything but for You to come and dwell in our city in all Your fullness. We just need a birth of Your Spirit to inhabit our community."

The Shunammite woman noticed that the man of God passed by frequently, and she acted on what she perceived God wanted. This book is a call to action for those who recognize the times we are in.

Gail Henderson is a woman much like the Shunammite. She is affluent and, like that woman in 2 Kings 4, her physical needs are taken care of. But she has a burden to see Jesus inhabit her neighborhood. Through her influence, she is helping hundreds of other women have an impact on their neighborhoods in Tampa Bay. Here is part of her testimony:

> **I believe that we can create a habitation for Jesus that will be irresistible.**

I was watching Charlie Brown's Christmas special on television with my sons one night, when I sensed the presence of the Lord. I began to weep silently at the sweetness and power of the Christmas message spoken out by children. I felt compelled to stage the same simple play in my front yard inviting neighbors and friends. Jesus must have had a front-row seat because people were touched and, during the next few years, we had to write in more parts as neighborhood children returned with their friends. We started with a makeshift stable, bathrobes as costumes and small crowds of relatives, but we quickly expanded to microphones, re-useable costumes, live animals and crowds of two hundred to three hundred people. Other neighborhoods began using the play with great results. My greatest thrill was to hear international women asking for the script so they could do the play in their countries.

During this time, we tried to take an interest in the people on the street. We held a few block parties, venturing into the realm of hospitality. I was being groomed for an opportunity, which became Florida's "Love Our Neighbor" coordinator, a friendship evangelism lifestyle marked by prayer, kind deeds, hospitality and gentle outreaches. I came to realize that where I lived was no accident. I had been handpicked (and so are you) to make a difference where I lived.

25

Interestingly enough, at that time I had little interest in tea but found myself fascinated with the subject and how popular and relational tea is for women. I did not know God was going to use that to encourage women all over the U.S., and now the international field, to use tea to meet and/or evangelize their neighbors. I began with one tea booklet (a booklet on how to use neighborhood teas to build relationships and, ultimately, share Christ) and added three more. We have had people saved at Christmas teas. People just meet each other. The response in the city to this sweet way to make new friends has been very positive. As a result, we have started Bible studies and currently have more than three hundred women who have adopted their neighborhoods.

Just as Gail had a burden for her city, Jesus had a burden for cities of His day, especially Jerusalem. Remember that Jesus tells the religious leaders that Jerusalem will be left desolate, as it was. But before that happened, Jesus embraces the city one last time. The book of Acts tells of thousands being saved and of the healing and deliverance that was taking place daily. Jerusalem witnesses the ministry of all believers, not just the apostles. In fact, the followers of Jesus act so much like the Master that they are called "little Christs" or "Christians" (Acts 11:26). Believers sell their houses and lands to take care of the needy among them—and there were no tax write-offs in those days (see Acts 2:45; 4:34–37)! All this takes place because His followers come together with one mind and of one accord and obey. What God does at Jerusalem He has done before and will do in the future.

Consider the example of Nineveh. God announces judgment on this city, but before it is destroyed He uses Jonah to bring revival. The great city of thousands of people repents and puts its faith in Jehovah God. Today many religious leaders, such as David Wilkerson, prophesy about the coming—some say current—judgment of America. Billy Graham is quoted as saying, "If God does not destroy America, He will have to apologize to Sodom and Gomorrah."

26

Do America's cities deserve to be judged for their sins? Possibly. But I know one thing for certain: Before God brings judgment, He wants to bring one last great revival that will yield the greatest harvest of souls we have ever seen. Jesus wants to embrace America's cities one last time. Do you perceive it? Will you act upon it?

3

"WOW" or Woe?

As we serve each other collectively, we invite Jesus to bring His WOW to our cities of woe. Let me share from the Scriptures what WOW means and Christ's desire to bring it.

We have seen how, on His way to Jerusalem, Jesus desires to embrace other cities as well. We read in Luke 10:1 that He sends seventy disciples "ahead of Him to every city and place where He Himself was going to come."

The seventy are to go out and prepare the way for Jesus in those cities, which line the path to His ultimate destination, Jerusalem. He gives them specific instructions in verses 8 and 9:

> "Whatever city you enter and they receive you, eat what is set before you; and heal those in it who are sick, and say to them, 'The kingdom of God has come near to you.'"

Notice that Jesus says, "Whatever city you enter and they *receive you*." By that, I believe, He means that whatever

29

city truly welcomes them is also receiving or embracing Him; they must, therefore, heal those in it who are sick. In other words, whoever receives them is receiving His Kingdom. Thus the disciples are directed to pass along a WOW. A WOW is simply a work of wonder. Jesus orders the disciples to heal those who are sick and do miracles in that city. And do it in the name and the authority of the King of the Kingdom of God. Jesus is saying, "Every city that will embrace Me, I will embrace with WOWs." Works of wonder are something we, the Church, can do and the world cannot. It may be a miracle healing or it may be a loving, unselfish sacrifice, but it is something that the world can look at and say, "Wow!"

An example of a WOW given to a city is seen in the testimony of Bill Craver, president of the Tampa Bay Dream Center ministry:

It was the spring semester of 1999 and I was on my way to school. We had just moved to Tampa and I had a thirty-minute drive to campus, where I was a teacher. Unfortunately it meant traveling the most congested freeways during the morning rush hour.

As I approached the city and saw the backed-up traffic, I decided to take a faster, side route. As I drove, I noticed there had been a major transformation of this area since I had traveled this way. Where there were once vibrant businesses and quaint neighborhoods was now a place of dilapidated stores and a prevailing darkness.

In the days to come, I felt a strange desire to take this same route. As I drove through what most people would call the ghettos, the Lord began to speak to my heart. I felt Him saying, *Look, see the fields.* Then God said, *Look with My eyes.*

I remembered a couple of friends who took meals to the inner city. My family and I volunteered to hand out meals. We were deeply moved by the spiritual climate of hope-lessness and despair. I was more determined to help. So I started attending city meetings on helping the urban poor. As I became more aware of the problems, my family and I became more involved by prayer walking various areas of the inner city.

At this time, high school students in my church had started weekly prayer-evangelism walks. They agreed that we were being led to an area called Ybor City. This is an area that is filled with nightly debauchery and neighborhoods filled with the poor and destitute. When the young people started prayer walking, they started believing God to provide a place of operation. We decided to lease an old wood-frame house that became our outpost. Once a drug haven, this house would now be a stronghold for the Lord.

My son, David, and four brave adults moved into the outpost and began to love the surrounding people. They held block parties and made meal runs to shut-ins. Help came when an area paper wrote an article on how five teenagers were changing the climate of a drug-infested area. When the article was printed, financial help and provision came, and we became a community effort.

As local residents observed our unified service to them, they realized that we were there not serving our agendas. They have adopted us into their hearts, minds and lives and the spiritual climate has changed the bleak despair of evil to the healing light of Christ.

Presently the little outpost has grown into a large outreach ministry called the Tampa Bay Dream Center where we minister daily to the needs of the community. Our mission in life is to help people find purpose and fulfillment by reaching into the inner city.

Many of those whose lives have been changed by the Craver family and the Dream Center team are now doing the serving in Ybor City. Our obedience to the still, small voice of Jesus through the Holy Spirit is God's way of saying He wants to bring a WOW to your neighbors and community through you.

Say No to Woe by Saying Yes to WOW

Jesus had a different word for those who refused to hear His voice and obey:

> "But whatever city you enter and they do not receive you, go out into its streets and say, 'Even the dust of your city which clings to our feet we wipe off in protest against you; yet be sure of this, that the kingdom of God has come near.' I say to you, it will be more tolerable in that day for Sodom than for that city."

> Luke 10:10–12

Jesus says here that He will have nothing to do with those cities that reject Him. Great disaster awaits them. Jesus pronounces judgment upon those who reject Him and His miracles. He declares:

> "Woe to you, Chorazin! Woe to you, Bethsaida! For if the miracles had been performed in Tyre and Sidon which occurred in you, they would have repented long ago, sitting in sackcloth and ashes. But it will be more tolerable for Tyre and Sidon [Gentile cities] in the judgment than for you."

> Luke 10:13–14

Jesus wants to bring a WOW but these choose woe. Can you believe it? Who in his right mind would choose woe over the WOW? You and I have that opportunity today. Jesus is once again passing by our cities. He is looking for those who will say, "Yes, come in and dwell in our city. Bring the WOW of Your Kingdom that comes with Your presence."

The Church is responsible for the spiritual climate of a city.

Our cities are already experiencing woe; we need a WOW. We, the Church, have allowed the woe to enter our communities through our pride, selfishness and independence. The woes of crime, violence, teen pregnancy, racism, drugs and more are rampant in our cities. These are all the woes of sin. We, the Church, who are responsible for the spiritual climate in our cities, can bring about change. We can be agents of WOW, according to Jesus. Just as Jesus sends out the seventy, He gives us authority and commissions us to impart the WOW of His Kingdom. Through unity characterized by love, humility, brokenness and selfless service, we are saying to Jesus that we receive His Kingdom, His rulership and His presence into our cities. Our actions cry out and say, "Lord, give us Your WOW, we have had enough woe." By bringing the WOW, we become God's gift to our cities.

A Super WOW

When the various components of the Body of Christ work together, they can have a powerful impact for the Gospel. Tampa, for example, hosted Super Bowl XXXV on January 28, 2001. Not to be outdone, Tampa-area churches hosted a super event of their own that weekend—the "Supper Bowl." Working with Operation Blessing, more than 175 churches, ministries and businesses came together and distributed 120,000 pounds of groceries, 3 truckloads of clothes and 20 pallets of cookies. The event also included children's programs; youth and adult bands; an educational tent; a health tent; and sports clinics in baseball, football and basketball with Christian athletes sharing their faith. In all, more than fourteen hundred volunteers from the local churches, compassion ministries, intercessors, businesses and youth joined together to have an impact on the bay area.

And the results?

Despite the chilly temperatures (for Tampa) that day, about twelve thousand people came out to enjoy the entertainment, games, candy and food. But by far the most important result, the result that will last into glorious eternity, was the 1,210 souls who gave their lives to Christ that day. The decision cards they signed were entered into a database allowing all participating churches to follow up.

Kristine Hartland, a local financial advisor with one of the major credit card companies, was grateful to have participated, saying people at her firm were "awed" by the number of people helped, needs met and lives enriched, and they responded, "Thank you for letting us share in this experience."

Most of the local media covered the day's activities. Michelle Bearden, religion editor of the *Tampa Tribune*, and Channel 8 news reported how even an unbeliever could sense the presence of God in a park usually known for drug activity and crime. One man who works at a local flourmill took advantage of the blood pressure and diabetes testing along with free food and clothing but found something more: "This is God's love in action, you can feel it all over the place here. It's been overwhelming being a part of all the smiles and kindness." It was truly amazing that in one of the most drug- and crime-infested parks in Tampa, people could feel the love of God. God manifested His presence that day. And not only the Church but the city of Tampa said, "Wow."

The following year we approached the cities of Tampa and St. Petersburg with "Carefest—A Week of Caring." We let city leaders know that we wanted to "come alongside" and serve them. The mayoral staffs in St. Petersburg and Tampa were amazed: "Wow, that's a switch." Both cities were ready to invest time in the project because of the Supper Bowl. They knew we could do what we said we would do. They asked us to serve in the worst areas of their respective cities. In other words, we had the opportunity to literally bring the WOW to their woe.

Every project these cities gave us, from painting to planting, building to raking, was fulfilled. The "Serve Tampa Bay

Day" was done on both sides of the bay simultaneously. In addition, one hundred thousand care packages had been distributed the previous Saturday throughout Tampa Bay.

One business owner, Bart Azzarelli of Dallas One Construction, told his 125 employees that he would pay them time and a half for working that day if they wanted to volunteer. When the city officials heard that, they responded with a collective, "Wow!" Remember, the WOW happened because more than fourteen hundred businesses and individuals decided to WOW their city with God's love in a practical way.

> **Our obedience to love our neighbors and community sends a heartfelt message to Jesus that says, "Jesus, we need Your embrace, Your WOW."**

Our obedience to love our neighbors and community sends a heartfelt message to Jesus that says, "Jesus, we need Your embrace, Your WOW." One day, when you stand before God, I hope you will be able to say, "Lord, I did all that You told me to do to embrace You and bring Your WOW into our community." Obey the Holy Spirit as He prompts you to action. Your obedience or disobedience could determine whether you will live in a "would" or "would not" city, a community that will know the WOW or the woe.

4

Evil in the Eyes of the Lord

It is a tragic day, recorded in Judges 3, when God hands the Israelites over to their enemies because of their sin and lets the city of Jericho fall into enemy hands. The account touches issues amazingly similar to those in America and across the globe. We, the Church, have also sinned and as a result, the enemy, Satan, has infiltrated our communities. This chapter will look at sin in the Church and its destructive consequences for our cities. The solutions and how you can be a part of it will follow. Let's begin with Judges 3:12:

> Now the sons of Israel again did evil in the sight of the LORD. So the LORD strengthened Eglon the king of Moab against Israel, because they had done evil in the sight of the LORD.

The key phrase is *they had done evil in the sight of the* LORD, which implies that they do not recognize the evil in their own eyes. Because this evil continues undetected, the Lord sends them a wake-up call, allowing King Eglon to advance and subdue the City of Palms—that is, Jericho. Did the Moabite oppression act as a spiritual alarm clock and awaken them to the fact that something was wrong? Apparently not right away. In verses 14–15 we find: "The sons of Israel served Eglon the king of Moab eighteen years. But when the sons of Israel cried to the LORD, the LORD raised up a deliverer for them." Notice that it takes eighteen years for Israel to answer this wake-up call. But eighteen years later when they cry to the Lord, He is still faithful to raise up a deliverer.

It is easy to take potshots at Israel with 20/20 hindsight. The Church has also done evil in the sight of the Lord and it too has gone undetected, unconfessed, unrepented for a long time. As a result, our cities have been infiltrated by the enemy. In the Tampa Bay area, the city of Clearwater has been the international headquarters for Scientology for more than twenty years. St. Petersburg is known as the psychic capital of America and as one of the last cities rocked by race riots. Tampa is the national leader of what is called "death music" being propagated by Marilyn Manson. Pornography and strip clubs abound. And, of course, the Tampa area also has the typical crimes, teen pregnancy and drug problems that infest so many of our communities.

What is the evil that the Church has failed to repent of in our communities? It is the lust, greed, selfish ambition and pride that too often exist in our pulpits, denominations and fellowships, the very sins that so many decry in today's television evangelists. But there is a profound sin in the Church today that is perhaps less obvious: a lack of unity.

38

Lack of Unity Is Sin

The Scriptures point out that a lack of unity is sin. In the prayer of our Lord in John 17, Jesus prays for unity or oneness four times:

> "And I am no more in the world; and yet they themselves are in the world, and I come to Thee. Holy Father, keep them in Thy name, the name which Thou hast given Me, that they may be one, even as We are. . . . [T]hat they may all be one; even as Thou, Father, art in Me, and I in Thee, that they also may be in Us; that the world may believe that Thou didst send Me. And the glory which Thou hast given Me I have given to them; that they may be one, just as We are one; I in them, and thou in Me, that they may be perfected in unity, that the world may know that Thou didst send Me, and didst love them, even as thou didst love Me."
>
> verses 11, 21–23

Note in verses 21 and 23, the main reason that Jesus says we are to be one is so the world may know that the Father sent Him. The lack of unity, therefore, hinders the Gospel and hinders the knowledge of the Lord covering the earth. Hindering the revelation of God the Son on the earth is a sin.

There is only one people group on the face of the earth that can hinder the prayer of Jesus in John 17. It is not the Muslims, Buddhists or Communists. It is the people we call the Church, believers in the Lord Jesus Christ, who can hinder—or advance—the prayer of our Savior that He be revealed to the world.

I have had pastors tell me they do not have faith for this unity and city-reaching stuff. And there are probably twice as many who think so without saying it. How can you have faith for reaching your community when you are coming from a place of disobedience? Obedience feeds our faith. We need to put ourselves into a place of obedience—not to reach the city, but because it is right and because Jesus prayed for us to be one. Obedience will feed our faith and will have much more positive impact than disobedience.

Other Scriptures that underscore this point are Ephesians 4:1–16 and 1 Corinthians 1:10–13. It is Philippians 1:27, however, written by the apostle Paul to the Church in Philippi, that best demonstrates the point:

> Only conduct yourselves in a manner worthy of the gospel of Christ, so that whether I come and see you or remain absent, I will hear of you that you are standing firm in one spirit, with one mind striving together for the faith of the gospel.

Paul says whether I am with you or not, conduct yourselves in a manner worthy of the Gospel. Look closely as Paul describes the behavior that he is looking for: standing firm in one spirit, with one mind striving *together* for the faith of the Gospel. Paul is pointing out that to conduct ourselves otherwise is *sin*.

Guess what, Church? According to Paul most of us have not been conducting ourselves in a manner worthy of the Gospel. We have not been of one mind or one spirit. Rather than striving together for the faith of the Gospel, we have often been striving against one another. Oftentimes the Gospel has continued to expand on the earth in spite of us, not because of us.

According to Paul's guidelines, most of us are not conducting ourselves in a manner worthy of the Gospel.

Unity is the nature of God. He is a triune God—three Persons in one God. Jesus prayed that we would be one as He and the Father are one. To be one, therefore, is to emulate God. And it is a witness to a divided, uncaring world. When we have the potential to be like Christ in this way and yet fail even to attempt to obey this biblical mandate, we are in sin.

We have become self-sufficient with our own church bodies, buildings and budgets. We build monuments to ourselves in the name of Jesus. While chatting with a friend of mine about some recent ministry accomplishment, he said, "Remember me when you enter your kingdom." He was joking, of course, but it convicted me of my "I" pride that fills the leadership in the Church and trickles down to all its members.

The Root Problem Is Love

Disunity springs from a lack of love. The foundation of the Christian faith is the sacrificial love Jesus showed us. Demonstrating that kind of love is the way others recognize us as His followers:

> "A new commandment I give to you, that you love one another, even as I have loved you, that you also love one another. By this all men will know that you are My disciples, if you have love for one another."
>
> John 13:34–35

Believers often memorize John 3:16, "For God so loved the world. . . ." But right after they do, they should probably memorize 1 John 3:16 as well: "We know love by this, that He laid down His life for us; and we ought to lay down our lives for the brethren." Colossians 3:14 offers a related insight: "Beyond all these things put on love, which is the perfect bond of unity."

I was speaking with a mega-church pastor in our community, appealing to him to be a part of pastors gathering in his city. His reply was, "The pastors who are really into this unity thing are mostly of small churches and I don't have the time or see the need as they do."

aid, "You mean those small church pastors like Ted
__ard and Jack Hayford?" (Both pastor churches of
seven thousand-plus and lead unity efforts in their cities of
Colorado Springs, Colorado, and Van Nuys, California.) It
is not a matter of whether you are part of a mega- or micro-
church. The real matter is, What is the will of the Father
and Son? The Father's will is to see the prayer of His Son,
Jesus, answered; so the world will know *Him*.

Those of us who have children (I have six) have said to
them at one time or another, "Why can't you get along?" or
"Why can't you play together without fighting?" God the
Father asks the same thing of His children. "Why can't you
get along? I've done all I can. I sent My Son and He bought
you with His blood. I gave you My Spirit to change and unite
you. Why can't you work together for My sake?"

Good question.

The world asks the same question. A drunk on the street
will say to you, "Why are you preaching to me when you
can't even get along among yourselves?" Though this is an
excuse to divert us, it is still an obstacle to our witness.

Covenant of Unity

When we speak of unity, we are not speaking of "anything
goes." More than two hundred pastors in Tampa Bay signed
a covenant of unity that is now being adopted in part or in
whole by other cities. Here is what they are agreeing to:

> We believe Jesus Christ has one Church, His beloved Bride,
> for whom He gave Himself. The church of Jesus Christ in
> Tampa Bay is composed of many believers and congrega-
> tions throughout the city. Jesus has sanctified and cleansed
> her with the washing of the Word of God so that she might
> be presented to Him, a glorious church without spot or
> wrinkle.

Christ has committed the care, cleansing and preparation of the Bride to us as shepherds. Endeavoring to keep unity of the Spirit in the bond of peace, we solemnly and joyfully enter into this covenant, pledging that by God's grace we shall:

- Love God with our all, and the Church fervently, doing all things in love.
- Pray for and encourage each other and our congregations on a regular basis.
- Speak well of one another at all times, especially in our preaching and teaching, putting to silence those who would be used by the adversary to spread evil reports among us.
- Hold one another accountable in regard to lifestyle, integrity and devotional life, meeting together regularly.
- Keep the bond of peace with the Body of Christ by carefully receiving members who have informed their previous church leaders as to their leaving, seeking to resolve any conflicts to the best of their ability.
- Be real and transparent with one another, resisting the temptation to impress each other with our size, abilities or accomplishments.
- Advertise in a manner that is positive to the Body of Christ, and not self-promoting at the expense of other churches or ministries.
- Respect and pursue relationships with those of different beliefs, while seeking to cross racial and denominational lines by meeting at the Cross. We believe in the essentials: unity, reconciliation and, in all things, love!
- Follow the Good Shepherd's example by giving our lives for God's flock in the Tampa Bay area.
- Prepare the Bride for the return of the Bridegroom, Jesus Christ, by mobilizing our members and promoting area-wide strategies and programs designed to evangelize and impact our cities with the Gospel of Jesus Christ.

As you may gather, this is an attempt to forge unity with some teeth in it. Has it been "walked out" perfectly? No.

Can we improve? Yes. But it is a good starting place. (For practical ways to unite pastors in your city, see our special leaders' section in chapter 13.) Most importantly, the pastors can be put at ease that the central point of our unity is Jesus Christ as Savior and Lord. Our unity is not ornamental. It is not a token meeting you go to once a year. As Doug Stringer, founder of "Somebody Cares America" and a friend for the past two decades, says, "It is unity with a purpose."

One person can influence others to bring about unity. Businessman Frank Brocato and his wife, Linda, have supported pastors in the Tampa area for the past twenty years. Frank developed a heart for pastors and their families after helping restore a church damaged by a pastor's moral lapse. Knowing of the tremendous pressure upon senior pastors, Frank has reached out to them through annual retreats, support groups and quarterly gatherings for pastors and wives. Each year he sponsors an appreciation banquet for 75 to 100 pastors and their wives. Frank's main objective is simply to offer love and support and give them an environment where they can pray and build healthy relationships with other pastors.

And it has worked. The Brocatos' ministry paved the way for a ministry like Somebody Cares to help pastors join hands and assertively reach the community.

Christ's love demonstrated through the unity of His Church is not an option. Because we have regarded it as optional, Satan has rewarded our disobedience with serious problems in our cities. *We, the Church, have done evil in the sight of the Lord and our cities have been reaping the consequences of our disobedience.*

The Devil Is a Fatty

Pastor Leonard Lord of the Light of the World Tabernacle in New Port Richey, Florida, said, "The only power the devil has is that which we give him through division." When our family returned from Nigeria, where we had lived for a number of years in order to plant churches and develop a discipleship school, my heart was broken over the fact that Scientology had bought up much of downtown Clearwater, Florida, my hometown. As the weeks passed, I saw that the devil's thumbprint was on neighboring cities that make up the Tampa Bay area in different ways. It occurred to me that none of these things could exist if there was a united spiritual front among the churches in Tampa Bay. The devil had power in Tampa Bay through division.

The Bible tells us, in the Judges' story of Israel's crying out for deliverance from her eighteen-years' servitude, that King Eglon of Moab was a very fat man. This fat king is representative of a very fat devil. In our culture obesity is looked down upon, but not in other cultures. In Nigeria, for example, a slender man is often thought of as being a small boy. But if you are large, you are considered a big man. It suggests that you are doing weil and enjoying life. King Eglon of Moab was enjoying life. He was prospering as a result of the disobedience of God's people. Similarly the devil is getting fat because of our disobedience. In other words, he is growing in power and influence in our cities, churches and homes.

> "The only power the devil has is that which we give him through division."

The people of Israel were under the authority of their enemy's king and paid tribute to that king. We also pay tribute to Satan in several ways. It is manifested in higher taxes to pay for more prison facilities, for larger police forces, for counseling for teens . . . the list goes on. Yet the problems increase in spite of the increased spending to remedy them. The fat devil's influence continues to grow at our expense.

Notice also that Eglon brought in his friends, the Ammonites and the Amalekites. This is how the enemy works.

He has no satisfaction level. Unforgiveness leads to anger, anger to depression, depression to violence, violence to guilt, guilt to suicide. The enemy is not content to bring in one problem. He gets his friends and they all grow together in your community. The king of Moab oppressed Israel for eighteen years before she recognized her need for deliverance. We need deliverance from this fat devil who continues to grow in power and authority in our cities.

In the late 1980s and early '90s the church in America began to see her disobedience. Our barrenness began to break us. We began to recognize that the state of our communities and country was a direct reflection of the state of the wider Church. We began to cry out to the Lord, singing, quoting and praying God's words in 2 Chronicles 7:14:

> "And [if] My people who are called by My name humble themselves and pray and seek My face and turn from their wicked ways, then I will hear from heaven, will forgive their sin and will heal their land."

God's people began to cry out for deliverance. We began accepting responsibility for the state of our communities. It is our apathy, indifference, greed, compromise, selfish ambition, pride, lust, lack of love and unity that have given the enemy his way in our cities. Like Israel, it has taken years of losing ground to the enemy to wake us up and to bring us to a place of repentance and desperation. But the Lord is faithful even when we have been faithless. He answers the cry of the desperate. Next we will look at the beginning of the end for the fat devil. The Lord answered the Israelites' cry for deliverance and He will answer ours as well.

5

Giving Birth to God's Grace for Your City

I have had the privilege of being present for the births of my six children. I remember the events surrounding each birth well. But the birth of our younger son, Peter, was particularly memorable. My wife, Kathy, and I decided to deliver him at home with a midwife.

Like all of our children, Peter came quickly. He was a large baby (almost twelve pounds), and his delivery, though short, was an adventure. During the delivery Peter's head came out but his shoulders were too broad. The midwife tried to get one of his shoulders out, hoping the other would follow more easily. No luck. We had to act fast. The midwife told Kathy to get up on her knees, holding on to me, to see if the gravity would help bring the child out. Kathy stared in disbelief. "Are you kidding?" she asked. But with our help she made it to her knees. Her nails dug into my back. I did not have to say, "Okay, on the count of three give a big glory shout to the Lord." No, Kathy's yell was totally involuntary. She has a great pain threshold, but this scream was one like I had never heard before. But the scream and elevated position worked. In a few moments, which seemed like hours, Peter plopped on the bed in perfect health.

We, as the Church, must become so pregnant with the desire to see God move in our communities that our crying out becomes second nature. It cannot be orchestrated. The apostle Paul knew of such prayer that gives birth. He travailed for the believers at Galatia until Christ was formed in them. In the Old Testament, Hannah, though not pregnant at the time, was pregnant with the desire to give birth. Something in her told her she was destined to give birth to someone special. Possibly it was her name, which means "Grace," that gave her this hope. She knew she was not called to barrenness. She knew she was to experience the special grace of God.

You also need to know that you are destined to give birth in the spiritual realm. You have not seen its fruit, but you are pregnant with the very concept. In fact, you might say that you could do nothing else, because you have become pregnant with the things of God. As the time to give birth draws closer, your cry to God will become long, hard shouts.

Our God is the same yesterday, today and forever. We can rest assured that, though we have been faithless, He will be faithful. The dramatic story of Samuel's eventual birth (see 1 Samuel 1) is a picture of two kinds of churches that we will see in these last days.

In the story two women are involved. Elkanah, the priest, has two wives, Hannah and Peninnah. Peninnah has a number of sons and daughters, while Hannah remains barren. As was the custom, they would travel to Shiloh annually and worship the Lord. Barrenness back then, of course, was looked upon as a curse. The ability to have children was conversely a sign that you were blessed by God. So you can just see Peninnah strutting, even gloating, as she makes her way before men to offer her sacrifice. Hannah shamefully pulls up the rear. Hannah's barrenness, however, would turn out to be her blessing.

Peninnah births sons in the natural sense. But her sons, it seems, never amount to much spiritually. The names of Peninnah's sons are never mentioned in God's Word. Peninnah produces sons that look good to the natural eye and religious thinkers but do not amount to much eternally. She is also barren in the spiritual realm but does not recognize it.

It is interesting that the name *Peninnah* literally means "coral." Coral is found in a myriad of colors and is very beautiful to see. But coral is actually made up of dead fish skeletons. In other words, it appears to be colorful and alive but in its center it is dead. This is how we often are in the Church. We look good on the outside. We have learned how to do ministry. But too often, at the very core, we are lifeless. The problem is that we do not know it. We believe we are fine by the fact that we have buildings, programs and budgets. We have become self-reliant and confident. We fail to realize our need to cry out because we do not know we are in desperate need.

A Perceived Fruitfulness, a Reality of Barrenness

It is not a question of, are you producing? The question is, *what* are you producing? Some of our churches are growing or producing, but what are we producing? If what we are producing has little or no effect on our communities then, as Jesus said, "The salt when no longer salty is good for nothing." As you will see later, it is better to produce one son in the spirit than ten or, for that matter, ten thousand in the flesh.

> It is not a question of, are you producing? The question is, *what* are you producing?

Are you desperate? You would think by the moral and spiritual decline we see in America and Europe that the Church *would* be desperate. Looking at the rise of crime in every level of society, you would think we would be hounding heaven for deliverance. It is not happening as a whole. We are content to help our communities—just as long as we are meeting our budget and our needs.

In *Loving Your City into the Kingdom*, Jack Hayford shares an encounter he had with the Holy Spirit during prayer. God showed him that his city was being destroyed. This is what the Spirit revealed to him:

> You are not being told "Los Angeles will be destroyed," because this city is already being destroyed. It does not need a catastrophic disaster to experience destruction because the Destroyer is already at work. The toll you have recounted, which a severe earthquake might cost, is small in comparison to the reality that stalks this city every day.
>
> More than mere thousands are being speared through by the shafts of hell's darts, seeking to take their souls. More than 150,000 homes (not merely houses) are being assailed by the sin and social pressures that rip families and marriages apart. More havoc is being wreaked by the invisible grindings of evil power than tectonic plates could ever generate. A liquefaction of the spiritual foundations that alone allow a society to stand is wiping out the underpinnings of relationships, of righteous behavior and of healthy lifestyle.
>
> You are to pray against *this*—the present, ongoing, devastating destruction of the city of Los Angeles.[1]

Los Angeles is no different from other communities. Destruction is reigning and the Church is indifferent. We are the Laodicean church not because we have material possessions, but because those possessions have corrupted our minds and dulled our spiritual hearts. Like Peninnah we believe our numbers or our affluence is a sign of good standing with God, regardless of what is taking place in the community that surrounds us.

The early '90s, for example, saw the advent of "Promise Keepers" and other stadium events. But the momentum of these movements has come and gone, and our crying out has largely ceased. Instead we must fervently continue what was begun. We must cry out to God to give us the grace to see ourselves as we truly are, "poor in spirit," wretched, poor, blind and naked. Then perhaps He will also give us the ability to cry out and change so that we can once again change our communities and nation by demonstrating the Gospel of Jesus Christ. As Eddie Smith of "Pray USA" said, "In order to be change agents, we must be changed agents."

Barren to Broken

Brokenness is the place where God dwells. Isaiah 57:15 says,

> For thus says the high and exalted One who lives forever, whose name is Holy, "I dwell on a high and holy place, and also with the contrite and lowly of spirit in order to revive the spirit of the lowly and to revive the heart of the contrite."

As we realize our barrenness, our inability to produce spiritually, it should bring us to brokenness. It is in this place of brokenness where we realize that our barrenness has been a blessing. It leads us to an intimacy and knowledge of God we would have never experienced otherwise.

As I said, Hannah is in a blessed place spiritually speaking. Her barrenness brings her to brokenness and causes her to cry out in desperation. You can imagine all the natural herbs she uses and old wives tales she listens to in hopes of making herself fertile. But to no avail.

Like Hannah you may have tried many programs, good ideas and the latest wave of what the Spirit has been doing only to find your community unchanged. It may not even be a whole community but rather a friend or a relative that you yearn to see born again. You have tried but are still barren. Are you tired of the devil's taunts through his growing influence on our society? Are you broken over the lives he and his henchmen are destroying? Are you broken over the sin that has caused division in the Church and allows Satan liberty to wreak havoc on your community? Then like Hannah let us cry out in desperation, broken of all our abilities and our sufficiency, and fall on God totally. Crying out to God is a declaration that we are emptying ourselves and our resources. It says, "God, if you do not do it, it will not get done. I absolutely surrender."

Brokenness Leads to Surrender

Hannah's barrenness leads her to absolute surrender. What is her admission? She says, "Okay, God, I give up. I can't produce anything on my own. If You will just give me the privilege of having a son, he is Yours. Take him and do with him as You will."

God is looking for the Church, especially in America, to cry out in repentance for its apathy and pride. He is looking for a Church to cry out in brokenness and humility over its impotence to influence its communities. Finally He wants us to cry out in surrender to His Lordship.

I believe that the next move of God is going to be greater than anything we have seen or heard of. It will require completely surrendered lives to be entrusted with such an outpouring. Surrender will be seen as churches lay down their labels, their doctrines that are not essential to the faith and their promotions and say, "God, we can't do it! Give birth to a sustained revival in our land that will glorify You and You alone."

Surrendering to God as Lord means that Hannah will give up her son to Eli to train. As we come together we must surrender our "rights." We say, "Whatever You birth, God, it's Yours to do with as You will. I surrender my part. I will play whatever role You want me to play and will get out of the way where and when I need to. I will yield to another to take over as You see fit for the purpose and plans You birth. I invite You to *manifest* Yourself and Your power to change my city."

> **"Whatever You birth, God, it's Yours to do with as You will."**

As we yield to the Lordship of Jesus Christ, we will experience God's special grace to affect our community.

Submit to His Lordship; Experience His Grace

When Hannah surrenders completely to God as Lord, she experiences His grace. Grace is God's power and ability to do what we cannot do. By God's grace, Samuel is born; Hannah's destiny of experiencing God's special grace is fulfilled. Her destiny is tied to the nation of Israel because Samuel will become a prophet who transforms his country. Hannah's one son, birthed by the Spirit, did more than all the sons of Peninnah, birthed by the flesh. Are you satisfied with the perception of being fruitful, or do you want to see lasting impact in your community?

Do you lack spiritual fruitfulness? Have you tried to influence lives, see people saved, but are still without any sons and daughters in Christ? Your barrenness can be a blessing in disguise if you will allow it to bring about a cry of brokenness and total surrender to God so that you might see God's grace in your life and your city. As we surrender as individuals and as congregations, it will affect the destiny of our communities.

I referred to Old Testament examples of God's people crying out and God's response. A modern day example is in Uganda. Uganda was known as the Pearl of Africa. But corrupt leaders brought devastation to the land and its people. It was a literal case of throwing a pearl before swine. Ugandans were known historically as a people who made covenants with tribal gods through human sacrifice. This cultic practice unleashed a spirit of death and destruction over this lush country. The repressive leadership of Idi Amin Dada, Milton Obote and others left the common man in daily fear. On top of this the World Health Organization declared that by 1997, one-third of the population would be wiped out through AIDS. They experienced a total economic collapse.

In 1984 the military was assigned to imprison, torture and kill Christians, and millions died. But persecution caused underground prayer meetings to spring up across Uganda. Churches across Uganda eventually began to *unite* in fervent, desperate prayer, travailing all night at times for God to end the death and destruction. God heard and opened the heavens over the Church in Uganda and it began experiencing a downpour of God's presence.

The presence of God was felt in prayer meetings throughout the country. Every zone and every community was praying. Pastor Jackson Senyounga's Christ Life Church grew from seven to two thousand members in a few weeks. Twenty thousand attend his church today. Many other churches also experienced Pentecost-like expansion. The following are some results from the downpour of God's Spirit on Uganda.

- The crime rate has dropped 50 percent.
- The economy, which was predicted to collapse, is now the third-fastest-growing of African nations.

- City-wide prayer meetings are commonplace, where they praise and thank God for the unity He has brought about.
- This AIDS epidemic is receding nationally, and people with full-blown AIDS are being healed miraculously. One pastor has reported 372 cases cured.
- Many national political leaders are standing for Christ.
- A new ministry of ethics and integrity has been established with a believer at its head.
- "Zero" tolerance for corruption has been adopted by the country.

During the country's millennium celebration in 2000, the President and the First Lady read a covenant, which proclaims Uganda as a country committed to the Lordship of Jesus Christ for the next one thousand years.[2] Just as it was God's will to see Hannah experience God's grace, I believe it is His will for whole communities and nations to live under His grace, as Uganda is experiencing.

I believe the apostle James was writing to individual believers and the Church corporately when he penned these instructions: "But He gives a greater grace. Therefore it says, 'God is opposed to the proud, but gives grace to the humble.' Submit therefore to God. Resist the devil and he will flee from you" (James 4:6–7). As we submit ourselves one to another and to the Lordship of Christ in our community, we are given the grace to resist the principalities, powers and spiritual wickedness in high places that seek to dominate lives in our city. Without this, we will be like the seven sons of Sceva. They tried to cast out devils without having the spiritual authority. The demons jumped on these presumptuous men, stripped them naked and ran them out of town in humiliation.

When we obey Christ and unify under His Lordship, the devil has to flee. He realizes that he is not dealing with First

United Methodist, Idlewild Baptist, Victorious Life Assembly of God or other churches. He is not dealing with individual congregations. He is being resisted by the Bride of Christ in that city. In other words the devil is messing with God's woman. The devil has to deal with the husband of the big "C" Church in your city. Not a good idea. Satan is no match and he knows it. He will flee.

> **As the Church unites, she, the Bride, can count on her Husband to defend and protect her.**

Do you want more grace? It is going to take God's grace to cut off the enemy's influence and power. I believe we will experience that grace as we submit to God by submitting to one another. God wants to give birth to revival in our cities. Jesus is looking for a submissive, obedient wife (Church) in your community. As we, Christ's Bride, become the submissive partner, our Bridegroom Jesus will produce through us more than we thought possible. Once the Church is submitted and pregnant, crying out for delivery will not need to be orchestrated. An obedient wife will allow herself to be inconvenienced with pregnancy and willing to go through the pain of delivery. Why? Because she wants to birth a baby.

Cry out for God to birth His power and presence in your community. Once something is birthed, yield it completely to God just as Hannah did with Samuel. Eventually you will be able to join in saying, "My city was doing evil in the eyes of the Lord, but when the Church in Cleveland, Tacoma, Phoenix, (your city), cried out, *then* God. . . ." Crying out is what all heaven is doing and what we will do if we want to bring heaven down to earth. God's will is that we cry out on earth as is done in heaven. Revelation 7:9–10 declares:

> After these things I looked, and behold, a great multitude which no one could count, from every nation and all tribes and peoples and tongues, standing before the throne and

before the Lamb, clothed in white robes, and palm branches were in their hands; and they cry out with a loud voice, saying, "Salvation to our God who sits on the throne, and to the Lamb."

The goal for Christians is to affect the earth with as much of heaven as we can before we go there ourselves. To do so we must cry out as Hannah did if we want to go from barrenness to fruitfulness. Crying out on earth is the will of the Father.

Revelation 11:15 says, "And there were loud voices in heaven, saying, 'The kingdom of the world has become the kingdom of our Lord and of His Christ; and He will reign forever and ever.'" If we are to see the change we desire, we must recognize our barrenness and the sins that may have caused it. This may be the corporate sins of the Church. As you identify with them, God will honor your humility. Let barrenness bring you to brokenness and begin crying out to God. Remember: Brokenness is where God dwells.

> The goal for Christians is to affect the earth with as much of heaven as we can before we go there ourselves.

This brokenness brings us to yield completely to the Lordship of Jesus Christ so that we may experience His special grace. Grace is where His power and presence births and sustains transformation in your community. With egos and agendas aside and Jesus as the Head, biblical unity and scriptural revival can take place. And that is where our next chapter leads us.

6

Unity Is Our Deliverer

Edward Miller, a missionary to Argentina, helped lead the revival that swept that nation more than forty years ago. Argentina was changed from a spiritual desert to a place of revival, where stadiums with seating capacities of 180,000 overflowed with people attending revival services. But it all began with fifty students from the Argentina Bible Institute crying and repenting on behalf of their country for 49 days straight.

Dr. Miller said: "If God can get enough people in an area to reject the rulership and the dominion of Satan, if enough of His people will reject Satan's dominion in the right way—with humility, with brokenness, and with repentant intercession, then God will slap an eviction notice on the doorway of the ruling demonic power of that area. And when He does, then there is a light and glory that begins to come."[1]

This story illustrates how God will raise up a people unified with the purpose of seeing deliverance come to a church, city or nation that is under the dominion of the kingdom of darkness. God did just that for the Israelites in Jericho in our story from Judges 3 mentioned earlier: "The LORD raised up a deliverer for them, Ehud the son of Gera, the Benjamite, a left-handed man" (verse 15). The Lord raised up a deliverer for Jericho, a man named Ehud, whose name means "Union." Now, as you read my testimony, you will find that this story has implications for us and our communities.

When we came back from Nigeria, our family settled first in Texas, but we wondered whether or not we should return to the Tampa Bay area. On several visits to my hometown, we pondered the negative changes that were taking place. Seeing the enemy's work there gave me a renewed burden for Tampa Bay. But I wanted more than a burden; I wanted specific marching orders and instructions from God. We had spent five weeks in the bay area but had not heard a clear word from God that we should resettle there after a twenty-year absence.

I was set to speak at a Sunday morning church service. We would be going back to Texas the next day. A few minutes before I was to speak, the Lord nudged me to look up what the name *Ehud* means. I had preached from this passage before about the left-handed man who slew the fat king but never thought to look his name up until that moment. Kathy had an *Open Bible* that gives the meaning of names. As my eye fell on the word and its meaning, it hit me like a load of bricks. *Ehud* means "union." The Lord spoke to my heart, saying, *Just as union delivered the city of Jericho, unity is the deliverer for your city.* In fact I understood that unity is the deliverer not just for my city but for all cities. We extended our stay for another week and I received a few more opportunities to minister this message.

> **The Lord made it clear that unity is what delivers a city from the enemy's hands.**

We went back to Texas and put our property up for sale. It sold in a month and we headed back to the Tampa Bay area. We had no financial backing from a denomination or church agreeing to support our family. We came with only one asset, which was, "God said."

This was December. I contacted some intercessors and shared the vision with them. They began to pray for its fulfillment. I began to reach out to pastors in Tampa Bay. About a month later we had our first meeting with about thirty pastors attending. God had gone before me and deposited the need to work together in their hearts.

By March we had three meetings taking place in different cities in the Bay area. By June the pastors had put together the covenant of unity. Burdette Price, a local pastor, hosted a program on the local television network. He arranged for the covenant signing to be done in the Channel 22 studios. The station later agreed to tape it and run it as a part of their programming. The initial airing was so popular that they ran it four or five more times.

Doug Stringer was getting national recognition for his efforts in Houston with "Somebody Cares America." Three hundred pastors and ministry leaders had completed forty days of prayer and fasting. It was having a ripple effect across the city. Doug had a vision to see the Somebody Cares concept go across the country. We were already implementing many of those concepts and developing some new ones. That night 126 pastors and ministry leaders signed the covenant of unity, and we officially adopted the name "Somebody Cares Tampa Bay."

Doug and I agreed to join forces; the leaders adopted "Somebody Cares" as their banner. We believe it is more than a name but a prophetic message. Our communities need to hear the church say, "We care because Jesus cares." Churches and ministries want people to know that somebody cares in their cities.

Like in Jericho, God raised up the deliverer, Union, in Tampa Bay. It is interesting that the deliverer was among the Israelites the whole time. The deliverer for our cities is among us as well. Deliverance is possible as we are in union with the Head of the Church, Jesus Christ, in our local communities.

I believe God still wants us to be the head and not the tail, but that will only happen as we come into obedience and union with the Head of the Church, Jesus Christ. Will we no longer be the tail? What does the head, as opposed to the tail, look like? The head is when local government leaders ask area pastors for their counsel, saying, "Please come to our meetings and give us wise insight on how to build and run our communities." By contrast, when a pastor is merely asked to come and do the opening prayer and leave so others can do business, that is being the tail.

> **We will only be the head and not the tail when we come into union with Jesus, the Head of the Church.**

We will only act as the "head" when we come into union with Jesus, the Head. Psalm 133:1 tells us: "Behold, how good and how pleasant it is for brothers to dwell together in unity!" My paraphrase of that verse is: God the Son, Jesus Christ, the Head of the Church, says, "True unity puts a smile on My face." You can be united but not have unity. You can tie the tails of two cats together and they will be united, but they will not have unity.

God is not looking for uniformity, where everyone is alike. The apostle Paul poses an insightful question in 1 Corinthians 12:17–20:

> If the whole body were an eye, where would the hearing be? If the whole were hearing, where would the sense of smell be? But now God has placed the members, each one of them, in the body, just as He desired. If they were all one

member, where would the body be? But now there are many members, but one body.

True unity celebrates each other's distinctive qualities as we celebrate Jesus, who brings us together as a bouquet of God's people.

Unity Brings God's Commanded Blessing

Psalm 133:3 ends by saying, "For there [the place of unity] the LORD commanded the blessing—life forever." Just imagine a scene in heaven. God looks throughout the earth, and of all the communities, the love and unity in yours catches His eye. You have become as irresistible to God as the Shunammite woman was to Elisha. Jesus says to the angelic host, "Behold I see that which is good and pleasant in My sight. Blessing, go visit the church of that city." When the Lord commands a blessing that blessing has to go.

Second Chronicles 16:9 says, "The eyes of the LORD move to and fro throughout the earth that He may strongly support those whose heart is completely His." If God's eyes are going to and fro looking to support an individual whose heart is fully His, how much more will He fully support a people in a community whose hearts are united for Him! The blessing is He, Himself. His favor comes in many ways, including physical, as His presence and power are manifested in the city through the Church.

The purpose of unity and the blessing that comes with it is "life forever." Its purpose is not to have endless unity rallies and unity bless-me clubs. It is not coming together to come together but uniting with the purpose of bringing "life forever" to our communities to set the captives in our city free.

Think about that last verse in Psalm 133. If God commands a blessing at the place called "unity" and we fail to make an honest attempt at biblical unity we are saying: "I'm okay with living outside God's commanded blessing for my community, church and life. I am not all that concerned about the fruit of unity—many more lives coming to know Jesus as Savior and Lord."

You may think, *I would never say that*. Maybe not with your lips but what do you say with your actions—or lack of them? I hope you are someone who will say, "Lord, I don't want to live one more day outside Your commanded blessing. Speak to me and show me how I can help bring about the type of unity that will command Your blessing and life forevermore for my community."

What most of our cities are experiencing is this: the Church willing to live outside of God's commanded blessing. This is why the devil keeps getting fatter and dominating the lives of our cities.

Unity: Wars Cannot Be Won without It

Jesus said, "If a kingdom is divided against itself, that kingdom cannot stand" (Mark 3:24). Satan's strategy is to divide God's people and make them as ineffective as possible in winning the people in their city to Jesus.

Read what Paul wrote to the Church in Ephesus:

> I pray that the eyes of your heart may be enlightened, so that you will know what is the hope of His calling, what are the riches of the glory of His inheritance in the saints, and what is the surpassing greatness of His power toward us who believe. These are in accordance with the working of the strength of His might which He brought about in Christ, when He raised Him from the dead and seated Him at His right hand in the heavenly places, far above all rule and authority and power and dominion, and every name that is named, not only in this age but also in the one to come. And He put all things in subjection under His feet,

64

and gave Him as head over all things to the church, which is His body, the fullness of Him who fills all in all.

Ephesians 1:18–23

I gather that Paul is saying that the rule and dominion of Christ should be ever increasing "in this age" as well as the one that is to come.

We should be experiencing an increase of God's rule on the earth—not a decrease. We should sense America turning from idols to the living God in greater measure than ever before. Instead we see darkness ruling the day. Why? Is there insufficiency of power and authority that Christ has bestowed on the church? No! The problem is explained in verse 22 above.

A modern day reality of the Scripture could read, "And God put all things in subjection under Jesus' feet, and gave Him as head over all things to the Baptists." Right? No! "To the Methodists?" No! "Assemblies of God?" No! You name the denomination or fellowship. He did not give all authority to one group or portion of the Church. He gave it to the Church. We have all authority and power if we truly work as different parts making up a greater whole.

Note in Judges 3:13 that King Eglon of Moab knows he will need strategic alliances to conquer the city of Jericho. He aligns himself with the Ammonites and Amalekites. In the past, they had been enemies, but they come together against a common foe in the Israelites of Jericho. Something similar happened in the closing hours in the life of Jesus when "Herod and Pilate became friends with one another that very day; for before they had been enemies with each other" (Luke 23:12). If the enemy is at work to create partnerships, God's leaders must do the same. There are partnerships within movements in the city and alliances with national ministries that help the local groups. We have such an alliance with "Operation Blessing." They truly come alongside the local work to help us reach the city. Ezekiel 7:23 says, "Make the chain, for the land is full of bloody crimes and the city is full of violence." Pastor Leonard Lord of Light of the World Tabernacle has often used this verse to encourage pastors to realize that we need to link up and form a chain to bind up the work of the enemy in our communities.

An army of one never won *any* war. You can build your mega-church of thousands while millions in your city go to an eternity without Christ. Let God use you to build a mega-church of thousands and to bring health to other churches in your city so they can reach collectively the tens of thousands if not millions.

Unity: The Job Is Bigger than Any One Church or Denomination

A quote I have often shared among the churches in Tampa Bay touches on the dimension of the job: "The Kingdom work in Tampa Bay is bigger than any one of us, so it needs everyone of us." This story from Jewish folklore, drawn from the Archko Volumes, helps make my point:

> "The Kingdom work in Tampa Bay is bigger than any one of us, so it needs everyone of us."

Jacob had twelve sons who were constantly fighting amongst themselves. One day Jacob gathered his sons together and told each of them to go bring him a stick. After each one returned with a stick, Jacob tied the sticks into a single bundle. He then placed his sons in line and gave the bundle to the eldest son and told him to break the bundle, which he could not do. Jacob repeated this test with all of his sons, from Reuben, Simeon and Levi down through Dan, Gad and Joseph. No one could break the bundle of sticks. Jacob then unwrapped the bundle and gave one stick to each son and commanded they break the stick, which they did easily. Jacob told his sons that they should learn two lessons from this. First, that which is bound together cannot be broken and, second, what they could not do alone, they all accomplished together.

There is no way one entity can do the job alone. There are key players everywhere, not only among the pastors but also among businesses, civil leaders, youth and prayer ministries. One of the things we have tried to do is to mobilize these key components of the Church for effective city reaching.

Unity: The Church at Its Best

Recently I saw this message on a church sign: "The world at its worst needs the church at its best." Well said. We can never be at our best if we are separated and disjoined. The first female bishop in the African Methodist Episcopal Church, the Rev. Vashti Murrhy McKenzie, said, "The Church is the center of the community and, as such, serves as a resource and a refuge, a hiding place, a helping place, and a healing place. What the community does not provide, the church stands ready to provide."[2]

Bishop McKenzie captures the Church at its best. We are called to be the blessing, God's gift to our cities. Although each congregation carries with it its own innate, God-given ability to be a blessing, we can never give God's best separately. Just as one member of a congregation can be a blessing and a gift, the members collectively bring abounding blessings and God's best.

Here is a story that shows the importance of the individual to the greater whole. My daughter Bethany joined others in doing "servant evangelism," where we give out free stuff to show God's love in a practical way. On Father's Day we were passing out packs of gum in front of a K-Mart. A few hours and a thousand packs of gum later we went home. The next week we learned that one of the recipients of Bethany's love gift was the regional vice president of K-Mart. He wrote:

> I just wanted to drop a quick line to say thank you for the little girl handing out candy and wishing all dads a Happy Father's Day. It made my day.
>
> I was visiting the store for an early afternoon check for K-Mart and found her to be delightful. I am not close to your church, since I live in Parrish, Florida, but you are doing a great job.

Since then this vice president has given us the green light to do free gift-wrapping at all 27 K-Marts in his region. One young girl's obedience to do servant evangelism with her group will now result in the church influencing thousands of lives during the Christmas holidays through free gift-wrapping.

Together we can be the gift (and sometimes the wrapping) to our communities that God intends us to be. We can pool the material and spiritual resources we have to be a blessing and bring down even greater heavenly blessings upon our communities. By doing so, as Bishop McKenzie said, we provide what the community cannot provide. Ultimately as they see the loving hand of God on their community, they will turn to Jesus and be a part of the solution and not the problem.

The Body cannot function at its optimum potential with some of its body parts missing. Paul told the church in the city of Corinth, "The eye cannot say to the hand, 'I have no need of you'; or again the head to the feet, 'I have no need of you'" (1 Corinthians 12:21). Again, what we would never say with words we show with our actions. We are so independent. We have our buildings, our budgets, our doctrine and our bodies. We have need of no one else.

We can never be our best apart from one another; we will be just like a body with missing parts. The Holy Spirit wants to bring us into conformity with the image of Jesus Christ. Jesus made it so that this conformity into His likeness could not take place outside a relationship with the rest of the Body. The Gentiles still want to see Jesus. The best likeness they will ever see on earth is through His Body, which the Bible calls the Church. But it will not reflect Him or point to Him unless all the Body parts work together. Scripture confirms this in Ephesians 4:15–16:

God will answer our prayer for deliverance as we answer Christ's prayer for unity.

> Speaking the truth in love, we are to grow up in all aspects into Him who is the head, even Christ, from whom the whole body, being fitted and held together by what *every joint* supplies, according to the proper working of each individual part, causes the growth of the body for the building up of itself in love.
>
> emphasis added

The leader's first responsibility is to make the Bride ready, in quality and quantity. When all the parts are joined together, dressed in love and humility, the total Bride in a city is beautiful. In fact it becomes attractive not only to others in the city but also to the Bridegroom, Jesus. If we are more concerned with being attractive to Jesus, the byproduct of that attitude will be that we will be attractive to others.

I will never forget at our wedding how the ushers had to ask friends of the bride to sit on the groom's side of the church. Her side was filled up and my side had plenty of room. It was not a slam at me. The fact of the matter is that the bridegroom usually is no match for attention on the wedding day. People come out to see the bride. You could hear the people chatting, wondering, "What kind of dress will she wear?" As my wife started down the aisle, teary-eyed women said, "She's so beautiful."

In the Old Testament, Ruth became irresistible to Boaz through her humble service. In a like manner we come together to serve each other, as well as others in our city. Together we become attractive to Jesus and our communities. We become irresistible to Jesus and He comes in the fullness of His Spirit to the Church.

Somebody Cares Tampa Bay is committed to seeing the Church in the Bay Area operate at its best—to love a world at its worst. We encourage people to love and serve one another so that the world at its worst will be attracted to Christ and His Church.

What are some ways to promote unity? Thanks to Renewal Ministries for offering 75 of these 80 ideas on building unity. Some may require your pastor's leadership. In that case, pray and then approach him or her. If your pastor fails to respond, continue to pray and do what you can.

1. On Sunday morning pray for another church to receive God's blessing. Send a letter to the church, stating the blessing.
2. Receive a love offering once a month for another church.
3. Provide funds for the pastor of a smaller church to attend a conference or seminar.
4. Provide money for a pastoral family other than your own to have a vacation they could not otherwise afford.
5. Conduct a series of concerts of prayer.
6. Have a "Serve (your city) Day." Pass out thousands of cold drinks and do deeds of kindness throughout the community.
7. If you are a pastor, swap pulpits with other pastors.
8. Invite a pastor or leader from another church to speak during your service about something exciting the Lord is doing in that church.

9. Invite a pastor or leader of a different denomination to lunch, just to visit.
10. Start a pastors' prayer group.
11. Establish a place of prayer in the community that could be prayed in 12 to 24 hours a day by people from different churches.
12. Encourage men in your church to participate in Promise Keepers events.
13. Conduct a "School of Prayer" for churches in your area.
14. Have an annual Thanksgiving service with area churches.
15. Ask area worship leaders to combine their talents and record a community praise tape.
16. Organize an outreach to place door-hangers, so you reach every home in your city.
17. Host a community concert featuring a Christian artist.
18. Enlist several congregations to meet at a different church on the first Sunday night of each month and worship together in the style of that church.
19. If you are in a pastors' group, invite the mayor or other civic leaders to be a part of it.
20. Host a civic leaders' prayer breakfast.
21. Organize various pastors in town to pray at city council meetings.
22. Create a 24-hour prayer room at a local hospital.
23. Draw up a "declaration of interdependence" and enlist as many churches as you can to sign it.
24. Have a prayer summit.
25. Have a community sunrise service on Easter in the Wal-Mart parking lot.
26. Organize a racial reconciliation banquet and use the proceeds to grant scholarships to children for Vacation Bible School at the church of their choice.

27. Study something like *Experiencing God* by Henry Blackaby or *The Purpose-Driven Life* by Rick Warren, together with another church.
28. Exchange Sunday school teachers with another church for one Sunday.
29. Work together to put on a community crusade.
30. Begin building cross-denominational houses of prayer in various neighborhoods.
31. Launch a corporate time of prayer and fasting for your city.
32. Do a combined-youth mission trip.
33. Have several churches pool resources to feed the poor during holidays.
34. Organize a city-wide food pantry to which all the churches contribute.
35. Make your building available to new churches that need a place to meet.
36. Send a group of skilled workmen from your church to do repairs on another church building.
37. Be willing to "loan out" leaders in your church to small or new churches that do not have money to support large staffs.
38. Send intercessors to various church parking lots on Sunday morning to pray for their worship services.
39. Put a list of all the city's churches and pastors in the prayer room to be prayed for daily.
40. Do a community church newsletter to report on what God is doing in the city.
41. Paint a sign for a church that does not have one.
42. Buy supplies for a new church.
43. Send your youth group to paint or clean a church of a different denomination.
44. Have churches pool resources to rent a billboard that advertises Jesus.
45. Meet regularly with the police chief or sheriff to get prayer requests.

46. Assign names of police officers, firemen, city workers, etc. to various churches to be prayed over daily or weekly.
47. Assign every public school to at least one youth group in town to pray for each week.
48. Start a community "Moms in Touch" group to intercede for teachers.
49. Set up a ministry network so that each participating church can focus on one ministry that it is called to. Each church would "tithe" to the others to support the ministries and would refer people accordingly. For example, one church would have an outreach for unwed mothers, one would distribute clothing, while another might run an adult literacy program.
50. Distribute the *Jesus* video to each home in the city. Attach a note that reads, "From the Church of (city), U.S.A."
51. Distribute Bibles in the same way, funded by all the churches.
52. Organize multidenominational prayer walks.
53. Make a commitment not to speak negatively about other churches.
54. Establish a sign, such as a candle in the window, for Christians to display in their homes as a reminder to pray for revival.
55. Encourage your church to hire staff members of other races.
56. Recommend other churches to first-time visitors.
57. Join up with churches to bless the city by renovating homes of the elderly and disabled and other community projects.
58. Share a radio program with church and business leaders from other churches that encourages reaching the community through unified efforts.
59. Rotate a cell phone prayer line among the churches.
60. Set up an interchurch prayer chain.

61. Support a community mission-outreach to the homeless.
62. Appoint a city-wide prayer coordinator to promote prayer and unity.
63. Do a joint revival, using local pastors.
64. Do a feature story in your church newsletter on a church not like your own. If you are a mainline church, for example, write a story on a charismatic church.
65. Conduct a solemn, city-wide assembly to repent of corporate sins, or a heal-our-land assembly.
66. Invite a group (such as music, drama, musclemen) to witness to the youth in the city. Hold the event in a public auditorium instead of your church.
67. Host quality seminars on worship, marriage, prayer, etc. and give discounts to people who are not members of your church.
68. Loan members to help start a new church.
69. If you are a pastor, preach a series of sermons on the strengths of other denominations and the importance of unity in the Body of Christ.
70. Formally commission and bless members who leave your church to go to a different one.
71. Send money to other churches' missionaries.
72. Sing the songs of another church.
73. Create an area-wide prayer map and distribute copies to all the churches in town.
74. Get with your neighbors who attend other churches and begin praying for the lost in your neighborhood.
75. Get with other believers in your neighborhood and throw a block party, Easter egg hunt, women's tea or Christmas pageant.
76. Adopt an inner-city church and begin to help them reach their immediate community.
77. Lend one of your worship leaders to a small church that has none.

78. If your community is racially divided, have a reconciliation assembly with resolve for action afterward.
79. Do a "Jericho drive" around your city.
80. Honor other churches with a unity award for their efforts in promoting and maintaining unity.

Please pray for wisdom and begin to implement one of these ideas. Share them with others and watch God open doors. God wants unity more than we do because He wants His Son, Jesus, revealed to a world enslaved by the devil.

We have seen that the deliverer, Unity, is already in your city. God will answer our prayer for deliverance as we answer Christ's prayer for unity. I hope that this discussion of four reasons why unity is our deliverer has motivated you to foster or be a part of the big "C" Church in your community. By doing this you will attract the manifest presence of Christ and have an impact for Him on those in your city.

You and your community have a destiny designed by God. The visionaries or leadership of the Church must understand the destiny of the Church in your community. They then must be willing to unify and serve one another to reach it. (See chapter 13, special leadership section.)

Once such leadership is established, it will be contested. As we seek to unify and mobilize Christ's army for our communities, it will not come without a conflict or fight. We all must come to a crossroads called Gilgal where we draw the line, stand and fight for our communities.

7

A Crossroads Called Gilgal

Ehud, the left-handed deliverer of Israel, faces a crossroads at Gilgal. He is confronted with the infiltration of the enemy into God's land, and he has to decide: Will he rise up and overthrow the enemy and see God's destiny for Jericho fulfilled? Or will he simply accept the enemy occupation?

The enemy's hand is at work in most of our communities. We can either be passive and accept it or rise up and see God fulfill His destiny for our communities. This chapter calls you to know your destiny and that of the community where you live. The challenge is: Will you pursue your destiny by cutting off every influence the enemy has to hinder your effectiveness?

Once God raises up Ehud, He then gives him a strategy for taking back the city. Ehud fashions a two-edged sword and straps it on his right thigh, under his cloak. The plan calls for assembling a special entourage to take the customary tribute to the king. When they hand him the tribute, they will assassinate him and then take back the city. At least that is the plan. But it does not happen that way.

> It came about when he [Ehud] had finished presenting the tribute, that he sent away the people who had carried the tribute. But he himself turned back from the idols which were at Gilgal, and said, "I have a secret message for you, O king." And he said, "Keep silence." And all who attended him left him.
>
> Judges 3:18–19

After delivering the money, Ehud and his companions leave the king's presence and start for home. Why the change? The timing may not have been right or their courage may have left them for a moment. But whatever the reason, they are on their way back home when they arrive at Gilgal. There, at Gilgal, something happens to Ehud that changes his mind and gives him the courage to go back. In fact the fear the others felt may have influenced Ehud, causing him to shrink back from the original assassination plot. He sends those accompanying him back home, and he goes to face the king alone.

What is it at Gilgal that makes Ehud do an about-face? Here is my opinion. In the history of Israel, Gilgal was the place where the Hebrews stopped before attempting to capture the city of Jericho. It is where God's promises to Abraham and Moses were fulfilled as they entered the Promised Land. At Gilgal the Lord spoke to Joshua, telling him to make knives to circumcise all the males born in the wilderness. Circumcising the males ratified a formal covenant between themselves and God. They would now be officially set apart as God's people and God would be their one and only God. The circumcision of the males' flesh represented their hearts being circumcised of all fleshly sins and deeds and being set apart to God. Gilgal became a landmark city. It was the place of preparation for one of the greatest victories in the history of Israel.

Not many days afterward, Joshua carried out the battle plan from the Lord to conquer Jericho and enter the Promised Land. Once each day, for six days, they marched silently around the city of Jericho. On the seventh day, they marched six times around in silence. Then they marched one more time. And on the seventh day, on the seventh trip around Jericho, the priests blew their trumpets and the people gave a great victory shout. The walls of Jericho came tumbling down and Israel possessed the city and, eventually, the Promised Land.

The word *circumcise* means literally "to make a circle." The men of Israel circumcised their flesh and their spiritual hearts and attitudes. Setting themselves apart to God, they then gained spiritual authority to "circumcise" the city of Jericho.

As they obediently circled the city of Jericho, they were circumcising it spiritually. In other words, they were cutting off the power and influence of the enemy over the city of Jericho. By the time they blew the trumpets and gave the great shout, the heavenlies were cleared. Their praise went straight to God's throne room. He received their praise, sent His power to prevail on the earth and brought the great walls of Jericho down. The key to this victory, however, actually occurred several days back when the male Israelites prepared themselves through circumcision. Gilgal was later used as their primary military headquarters as they continued on to possess the Promised Land.

Now fast forward to Ehud as he comes to the city of Gilgal. The city would again be the place where Israel, this time in the person of Ehud, prepares for great victory. Yet as Ehud approaches Gilgal, he sees what has become of it. The city where Israel had renewed her covenant with God and from which she went to great victory is polluted by idols (see verse 3:19). The Holy Spirit reminds him painfully of the glorious place Gilgal and Jericho held in Israel's history. It is then that the spirit of boldness and holy anger rise up within him. I believe he says at this point, "No matter what it takes, the Moabite king (the devil) cannot have my city. He cannot have Jericho." So he turns around and goes back to Jericho to face the challenge.

Your City's Present Reality Is Not Its Destiny

Jericho's present reality confronts its future destiny at a crossroads called Gilgal. America and its cities are at a similar crossroads: America's dark, spiritual reality today versus its true spiritual destiny. When we talk about cities we are actually talking about the many lives that make up that city. The lives of many people are at a crossroads as we seek revival and spiritual awakening to burst forth.

> America's dark, spiritual reality today versus its true spiritual destiny.

We need to rise up in our cities and draw the line. Mayor Carolyn Risher of the town of Inglis, Florida, literally told the devil that he could not have her town. This proclamation by the courageous mayor received national attention (see Appendix B). Make your own proclamation for your neighborhood or even your home. You might add a positive declaration as Joshua did, "As for me and my house we will serve the Lord."

Put the devil on notice in your community. A vigilant cry by God's people can have an effect, since God will hear the cry of the desperate. He has given us authority over the enemy. If we back our words with actions we will see less and less of the enemy's power and influence.

The Bible says that there is a time to hate (see Ecclesiastes 3:8). It is time to hate what the devil is doing to our communities, block by block, and it is time to take them back.

Elzie Mahoney, a local business owner, wanted to express to the public that his company was the Lord's. He decided to put the words *Jesus Is Lord* in bold print on his business sign. He arranged the lighting to spotlight his message at night. One of his patrons had been consistently praying for his lost son. Unknown to the father or Elzie, the son frequented a bar across the street from Elzie's shop. One evening as he left the bar, the sign caught the young man's eye. He walked across the street and kneeled down, yielding his life to Christ. Then all three men began praying that the bar would close, and it did. Your declaration may be on a sign you place in your yard. We have put out signs offering prayer in more than a thousand neighborhoods. These yard-sign declarations yield great results. These signs draw those in need, from neighbors, delivery people and other passersby.

> **America is at a crossroads, but God will hear us if we cry out to Him.**

It is time we come together and say, "We are mad at the devil and we are not going to take it anymore." It is time to fight the good fight and see God's Kingdom come and will be done in our communities. We have enough citizens of the Kingdom to bring about the transformation that God desires.

The name *Gilgal* means to "turn away reproach." Gilgal came to be known as the place of preparation for Israel's great victory at Jericho, the place where Israel turned away the reproach of forty years of wilderness wandering, brought on by disobedience. Its destiny was not to be a city known for false gods and idols. And Jericho's destiny? Its name means "city of palms," from which I get the image of a place of rest. Jericho was the place where the Israelites entered their rest as they crossed over the Jordan into the land promised to them by Jehovah God. It was not to be a place of oppression and unrest ruled by a devil named King Eglon and his friends.

There is even further significance in the place called Gilgal. This is where the children of Israel crossed the Jordan River—on dry ground. As a testimonial to God, the Israelites took twelve stones, actually boulders, from the Jordan River and mounted them together in their camp at Gilgal. Joshua declared that these stones would become a landmark for generations to come, a witness of God's faithfulness and omnipotence. Joshua 4:21–24 states:

> He said to the sons of Israel, "When your children ask their fathers in time to come, saying, 'What are these stones?' then you shall inform your children, saying, 'Israel crossed this Jordan on dry ground.' For the LORD your God dried up the waters of the Jordan before you until you had crossed, just as the LORD your God had done to the Red Sea, which He dried up before us until we had crossed; that all the peoples of the earth may know that the hand of the LORD is mighty, so that you may fear the LORD your God forever.

Joshua's proclamation was not the reality in Ehud's day. The area was laden with idols. You can imagine this scene taking place at Gilgal between a father and his son. The boy sees the pillar of boulders and asks, "What are these stones?" With great pride the father tells the story of how God caused Israel to subdue their enemies and cross the Jordan on dry ground, just as they had the Red Sea. Then he says, "These stones were placed here so that everyone would know and fear Jehovah God." The son replies, "That is cool, Dad, but if that's true, then what's up with all these idols?"

Can you see Ehud on his way back to Jericho? Perhaps he sees these stones or even overhears such a conversation between a father and son. Either way he is reminded of Israel's great past. He sees the landmark as a promise of Israel's future that has been stolen by the enemy and he rises up with righteous indignation to restore God's testimony in the land.

How about you? Have you seen God raise up a testimony of His love, mercy and power in your life only to see the enemy taint that testimony? Have the things of this world become idols in your life, discrediting the Lord's testimony and keeping you from reaching your full potential? Are our children getting mixed messages as to who is really ruling the land, our homes and our lives?

We can teach our children the history of America, that our forefathers intended this to be "one nation under God." Yet it has no real punch unless we are living our lives under God's authority and the subsequent blessing of His presence. As we stand and restore God's rightful place in our lives and homes, we once again become the people of impact and influence that Jesus said we would be.

God is not through with you, your city or your country. As we obey individually, one by one, we can cause a snowball effect and see a spirit of revival cascade upon our land. The God of the second chance is not through with you. The fulfillment of your destiny is on the way and, with it, the fulfillment of the church's destiny, to be God's gift to your community.

Your City's History Reveals Its Destiny

I believe that the history of a city reveals its redemptive purposes or destiny. The history of Tampa Bay, for instance, has given us insight into the redemptive purposes of God for our communities. Like Ehud, this insight has stirred us to action to see it fulfilled. In reading the history of Tampa Bay and the city of St. Petersburg, we found that Tampa Bay was originally named the Bay of the Cross and later renamed by the explorer Cortez in 1507 the Bay of the Holy Spirit. In our day the influence of a large church, Without Walls International, found favor with Mayor Dick Grecco and persuaded him to declare that Tampa Bay would be called the Bay of the Holy Spirit for one day. This is what God intended it to be called.

As I have already shared, the city of Tampa has become known as a leading producer of death music, which Marilyn Manson promotes, and also of pornography. St. Petersburg is known as a leading center of psychics in America and also a city of racial unrest or, as the African American community calls it, racial revolution. Whatever you call it, it is far from what God wants for St. Petersburg, a city named after the apostle Peter. The mayor of St. Petersburg, Rick Baker, a devout believer, has a vision of St. Petersburg as a "seamless city." In other words, a city with no division. Another major city in the greater Tampa Bay area is Clearwater, and it is known as the international headquarters for the cult Scientology. Much of what has been mentioned is the reality of Tampa Bay, but none of it is its destiny.

Yet God revealed to me Tampa Bay's true destiny, in spite of these manifestations of the enemy. From this bay area, various businesses have been birthed that have become national and regional franchises. Eckerd drug stores, Checkers, Hooters, Hops and Outback Steakhouse restaurants all had their genesis in the bay area. As I prayed and thought about Tampa Bay's destiny, I was reminded that what has taken place in the natural is indication and confirmation of what God wants to do in the spiritual.

> **Our cry became, "Lord, give us the Bay of the Holy Spirit, give us the nations!"**

The Holy Spirit birthed the Church two thousand years ago as He descended upon the 120 in the Upper Room in Jerusalem. As the Holy Spirit gives each of us our second birth, many spiritual leaders believe He wants to birth a move of His Spirit. I, and other leaders in Tampa Bay, believe that what has happened in the natural realm God wants to do in the spirit realm. He wants to franchise a birth—a move of the Holy Spirit. The Bay of the Holy Spirit's redemptive purpose is to be the birthplace of a move of God that will affect our state and the nation with a move of His Spirit. We borrowed a cry from Somebody Cares Houston: "Lord, give us the Bay of the Holy Spirit, give us the nations!"

An example of the unique birthing of the Holy Spirit is taking place in Tampa through Tommy Kyllonen and his ministry. Here is his testimony:

> When I was around the age of ten, the urban culture really began to take root in my life and I became a break dancer. In the years that followed, I also began to rap and became a street graffiti writer. Although I believed in God and was still made to go to church, I was definitely not living it. Although I made a lot of mistakes and hung with the wrong crowd for several years as a teen, God continued to keep his hand on my life. At the age of eighteen, I recommitted my life to Christ and decided to go to a Christian college. During my second semester, I got involved in a homeless ministry in the subways in center-city Philly. I also got involved as a helper in an urban youth ministry. Through this God showed me he was calling me to urban ministry.
>
> After graduation God led us to an urban church called Crossover Community Church in Tampa. It was a small congregation of about forty people that had never had a youth ministry before. Joe McCuthen was the founding pastor and had a heart to reach out to urban people who wouldn't fit in your more traditional type of church. We did outreach programs and basketball leagues in the local housing projects and neighborhoods around the church. By the end of the first year, we had close to fifty teens attending our weekly Thursday night youth service. Soon we began to raise up leaders out of the people we were reaching. Within a few years the youth ministry grew to more than one hundred teens, as more were finding out about our unique approach.
>
> We began to incorporate elements of the hip-hop culture into our worship service to make it more relevant to the crowd we were trying to reach. We began to use a live DJ, on turntables, during our praise and worship time. Instantly kids who never worshiped were connecting and beginning to praise God in

a relevant way. Several break dancers began attending and accepting Christ. Soon we started break dancing classes. We started MC classes for youth that were into rapping so we could help them develop their talents and use them for Christ.

The youth ministry continued to grow and began to get national attention. During this same time period, I put out two independent Christian, hip-hop albums and began to develop a fan base. This really opened many doors for our ministry to get known. Soon we were flooded with phone calls, emails and visits from people from all over the U.S. and beyond. We saw the need to start a conference to train pastors, youth pastors, leaders and hip-hop artists to reach our culture more effectively. The following year "Fla.vor," our annual hip-hop/urban ministries conference, was birthed.

Next I took over as the pastor of the church. The majority of the forty adults who attended on Sundays were there as a result of the youth ministry and the hip-hop concerts we put on every three months. God made it clear that He wanted our church as a whole to reach out to the hip-hop culture. Statistics show that fewer than 27 percent of people between the ages of 18 and 35 attend church. Out of the forty adults we had, most of them were in that bracket already, and we all knew that these were the ones we were called to reach. New vision and structure was birthed at Crossover, and God began to move in big ways. Worship services became more relevant, new ministries were started and many people were discipled and trained.

People around the world are now looking to us as a model of the first hip-hop church in the world. It's a huge responsibility. We are running out of space at our current facility and feeling many growing pains. There were more than 230 people at our Sunday worship service today, and more than 325 at our youth services this past Thursday night. You can find out more about our ministry and our conferences, which have more than 1,400 attendees, at www.crossoverchurch.org

God is using the bay area for birthing spiritual tools and initiatives to bless other cities such as Tommy and the hip-hop church. As I already noted, the collective inspiration and wisdom of the pastors produced a covenant of unity, which is now being adopted in part or in whole by other cities. A forty-day revolution of prayer and servant evangelism called "Operation Light Force" is going throughout youth groups in cities across the land. The late Dr. Bill Bright's "World Changers" radio program took forty minutes of testimonies from teens who saw God move in their schools. Another ministry that has gone national in recent years is "C12." It is a ministry to Christian CEO's started by Buck Jacobs. You will read more about it in chapter 10 on mobilizing the marketplace. Jerry Brandt, a local evangelist who has worked intimately with Somebody Cares Tampa Bay, received a tool to reach cities for the Lord. The campaign is called "Just Ask Me." He teaches believers how to write and share their own stories of how God saved them. Jerry figured out how churches can systematically reach their cities with the Gospel in a short period by using the program.

Another tool that was a part of our "Year of Answered Prayer" campaign was prayer boxes. Dr. Terry Teykl, who teaches and ministers on renewal and reaching cities through prayer, told me how a little old lady at a church where he preached came up to him and said, "We need to take those prayer boxes out from the back of the church building and get them into the marketplace." He thought it was a good idea and so did I.

We found a manufacturer who created "The Year of Answered Prayer" prayer boxes. They look like boxes in which you would place entry forms to enter a contest. Instead they have pads for prayer requests. Those boxes went into five hundred businesses all throughout the bay area. The concept now is being taken to other cities through Dr. Teykl's ministry.

The Christian Broadcasting Network was about to launch a national campaign called the "Book of Hope." They were looking for a well-networked community that could make a successful kickoff in about forty days. The network of churches through Somebody Cares Tampa Bay was the pilot prototype for forty other cities. They asked the churches in Tampa Bay to distribute these Gospel booklets to homes, using the attractive door hangers they supplied. They projected that we would reach approximately 250,000 homes, given that we had only one month to prepare. But we doubled that amount, distributing nearly 500,000 in one day, which we called "A Day of Hope for Tampa Bay." Little by little the destiny of the Bay of the Holy Spirit is being realized.

Another project birthed here and being duplicated in other major cities is called "Raise the Roof." Raise the Roof is an evangelistic concert held in conjunction with sporting events in Tampa Bay. The idea is now being adopted by sports teams like the Houston Rockets, the Comets and the Staple Center in Los Angeles, California. I will share on this more fully in chapter 12, "The Power of One."

Lastly the successful network of the Christian community fostered through Somebody Cares Tampa Bay has spawned Somebody Cares networks in other cities and other Florida counties.

The present reality of your city does not have to be its destiny. Leaders and individual members of God's church in your city must come to a place called Gilgal. Gilgal is the crossroads. It is the place where we collectively and individually say, "I'm not going to let the devil have my city." Almost every city has a destiny that is different from its present reality. In fact, your life may have a destiny that is different from your current reality. You must draw the line for yourself and for your city just as Ehud did. You must have the resolve that says, whatever it takes, the devil cannot have his way with my life, my city and the lives that are in it.

At Gilgal, circumcision took place. We must come to our Gilgal and cut away whatever would hinder us from obtaining our personal destiny in Christ. If we are going to make a difference in our world, then the Lord will start with us.

88

As we do so, we help to achieve the destiny of the corporate Body of Christ in our city.

As leaders we must allow God to break our hearts over the situations in our cities. We must take ownership of the present spiritual decay and darkness. We must ask God to do surgery on our hearts, so that nothing will hinder us from using the authority God has given us to cut off the enemy's power and influence in our communities.

> **The present reality of your city—or your life—does not have to be its destiny.**

The full purposes and destiny of your city cannot be realized without the embrace of Jesus. Your willingness to confront the devil and be loosed from his entanglement is a message of love that you send to the Bridegroom. You are telling Him that the Bride in your city is preparing for her eternal destiny through His everlasting embrace.

Like Jericho and Gilgal, Tampa Bay has a distinct destiny in God. We have learned how we must rise up in faith to expel the enemy's influence and see God's redemptive purposes prevail. Study the history of your community to discover what God's intentions are for it. Let God speak through the history, landmarks, etc. that define your city's destiny or at least its history. Also note the influence the enemy has in your city. Share what you find out with others. Ask God to bring His people together to pray and to take action to see their city changed from the present reality to God's destiny for the church in your city. As we rediscover our destiny as the capital "C" Church in our communities, we will find that God has given us a message to fight with to see that destiny become a reality.

Now let's see how God used Ehud to help fulfill one city's destiny.

8

A Message from God for the Devil

Perhaps you have seen the witty TV commercial in which an average Joe is sitting on his power mower wearing a tank top. As he begins to speak, rather than his voice, the voice of a young woman with rich taste, no money and a southern accent is heard. Her voice tells of the trips, jewelry, clothes and other luxury items she bought using the credit card she stole from Joe.

This is a humorous way to get our attention on a serious problem. The commercial then tells viewers how they can prevent identity theft.

Stop Identity Theft

Identity theft is no laughing matter. This is one of Satan's primary objectives: to steal, kill and destroy your true identity in Christ. He wants to steal not only your identity but also the intended identity and destiny of your community.

As with the commercial, you can vicariously hear the voice of the enemy. He says things like, "This guy was supposed to have a good job, a stable family and a great testimony for the Lord. I stole it all. I got him to commit adultery, and his wife left him. He got depressed and started drinking, then lost his job. I got him believing he can never amount to anything again."

This is true with whole communities. God's intentions for them are often not what they are identified with in their current state. Like Jericho and Gilgal, these communities were not to be identified as full of idols or dominated by a big fat king (devil), as previously noted. And neither is your community.

The only way to stop identity theft of an individual or community is to have that person or city find its identity through Jesus Christ. This is why we want Tampa Bay to be known for its original name. By being the "Bay of the Holy Spirit," we are finding our identity as a community through King Jesus and His Kingdom. Of course, in order to see this realized to its fullest we must see each individual do the same. This is why we have as one of our objectives to "Transform Tampa Bay," by touching every heart with the heart of God.

Satan's plan is to steal and to destroy the true identity of every one of God's creations. Our plan must be to see all people find their identity in Christ so that they can fulfill their God-given personal and corporate destinies. This chapter will tell us some means by which we stop the theft and walk in what God has for us individually and corporately.

Ehud once again entered the king's palace. His ticket for an audience was that he had a special message from the God of Israel for the king. The king was curious and unaware that Ehud posed any threat. The king ordered everyone out of the room, and Ehud delivered his message in the form of a two-edged sword that he thrust into the belly of the fat king. Then he slipped out, locking the doors behind him. After an embarrassing amount of time—the guards thought the king was relieving himself—the guards opened the doors to his chamber. "And behold, their lord was fallen down dead on the earth" (Judges 3:25, KJV).

It is Jesus who will ultimately put Satan away for good. But, spiritually speaking, we can cut off Satan's influence over the lives of people in our communities and cause that influence to die. There are strategies, tactics and tools for cutting off the enemy's power and reaching your city for Christ. In that regard we can learn from Ehud: God has a message for the devil in our communities as well. Just as Ehud used his double-edged sword to slay the enemy, so God's people must *unite* to use our two-edged sword of the Spirit: the written Word of God and the rhema word of God.

> **As we come together and seek God's face, the redemptive purposes for the city will become known.**

A rhema word is a prophetic word given by the Spirit of God to give us direction. The rhema word will always agree with God's written Word. This two-edged sword becomes a mighty weapon, cutting away falsehood that the enemy has used to cloak your community and applying the truth.

As we come together and seek God's face, the redemptive purposes for the city will become known. Faith will rise as we begin to see our communities through God's eyes. Through the Holy Spirit's leading we will learn tactics and strategies to bring about God's purposes for the city. An example of this can be found in Isaiah 62:4. Speaking of Israel, the prophet says:

> It will no longer be said to you, "Forsaken," nor to your land will it any longer be said, "Desolate"; but you will be called, "My delight is in her," and your land, "Married"; for the LORD delights in you, and to Him your land will be "married."

In this message, God gives the disobedient children of Israel a promise of their future. From it they draw hope that their present reality is not God's destiny for them. In other words, forget the past and what your current tag is because God is giving you a new name and calling you to a new destiny. In fact this new name has your calling and destiny within it.

Here is what we might proclaim for Tampa Bay: "Satan! The Church in Tampa Bay has a message from God for you. We are the Bay of the Holy Spirit! We will not be known for death music, leaders of pornography, racial riots, psychics and the headquarters for cults. We will not be a church full of wrinkles called division and spots of impurity. We will be a place of habitation for the Lord Jesus Christ by His Holy Spirit. We will be humble of heart and contrite in spirit because that is where the holy and lofty One promises to dwell. We will be known for birthing a move of God in America."

Dr. Terry Teykl, who is mobilizing United Methodist churches across America, writes about this power of agreement in his book *Pray the Price: The Power of Agreement*:

> [G]etting two or more pastors to agree about anything can be quite an accomplishment! We are an opinionated bunch. But in the economy of God, agreement yields results, and when a church or a city really takes hold of that truth, and applies it to their prayer life, miraculous things begin to happen.
>
> The Greek root word for "agree" . . . suggests a "symphony." Our prayers of agreement are like the harmonious blend of symphonic instruments offered up in behalf of a need. I illustrated this concept one Sunday morning during church by asking our musicians, without conferring with each other, to all play at once any song that came to mind. Of course, the result was discordant, chaotic noise. But when they were in agreement about what they were playing, though their parts were different, the result was a beautiful melody. It is pleasing to God when believers pray in harmony, on the same page. Though individually our prayers for this denomination may seem small and insignificant, imagine

what a magnificent symphony would be created if United Methodists of all persuasions were to pray in agreement for a spiritual awakening in our Church.[1]

How magnificent would that symphony be if the denominations would agree, or the churches in your city would agree, in prayer for those things that we believe would move God to bring a spiritual awakening to our cities!

As we declare jointly the true purposes of God for our areas, our declaration acts as a sword cutting into the spiritual belly of the enemy. He is defenseless against unified, persistently applied truth. We do not kill the devil but we can kill his power and influence over our communities.

After slaying the fat king, Ehud goes to the hill country and blows his trumpet (Judges 3:27). The trumpet represents God's call to His people, and the place from where God is calling His people is Ephraim. The name *Ephraim* means "fruitful." That is the call on the church in America. He is calling us to bear the fruit of changed lives in our cities. He is calling us to be a victorious, productive church.

This applies not only to the corporate church but also to the individual. Maybe you are someone who started out well in your faith in Christ but who has gotten sidetracked by the enemy. Possibly you have fallen into sin that has led to bondage. The enemy is getting fat off your life. The vices—drugs, drinking, gambling, pornography—are costing you financially. You have lost jobs over them. They may have even destroyed your relationships, marriage and family. You are paying tribute to the devil with your time and energy. You have lost your purpose and calling as a believer.

> He is defenseless against unified, persistently applied truth.

Take heart. God has a message for you to give the devil. It is found in your new name.

Using Your New Name

Pastor Brian Pierce's testimony is a great example of how God can give an individual a new name and calling:

> For more than 25 years I was a helpless, hopeless drug addict and a drug and weapon trafficker. My life of addiction led me many places at many different times, including jail nine times in five different states. Cocaine was my devil and money was my lover. My reckless life took a terrible turn for the worse when I was arrested in 1990 for interstate trafficking and transportation, possession and possession with the intent to traffic cocaine—an ungodly amount. I managed to find my way out of jail on bail. It wasn't the police I was running from, it was the Colombian drug cartel that was also busted because of my arrest. They put a hefty price on my head. I had found my way onto their hit list! After running from the police, the Colombians, myself and God for so long, it became overwhelming and I decided to kill myself rather than suffer through the shanty life I was living. It was then that God showed up.
>
> I have a new life now. After a year in Christian recovery, God called me by name and told me of His plan for my life. I attended Bible college and founded "Taking It to the Street Ministries" in St. Petersburg, Florida. Now I take God's Word to the lost and hurting. God opened my eyes to the pain and suffering of my city. I had a crushing burden to do something. Since then, with the help of my wife and many partners and helpers, we have led eleven thousand people to the Lord, opened two residential Christian recovery centers, help start four orphanages in Trinidad and help feed nine thousand meals a month to the homeless. God has created, called and chosen. He changed my life.

God has not called you to be addicted to drugs or alcohol. He did not die for you to be dysfunctional, depressed or incarcerated. He has called you to be fruitful. But you need to apply the Word of God. Because of your backslid state,

96

you are missing out on the true call of God on your life. Repent quickly and apply God's sword to your life. Romans 10:9–10 will work for you right now. It says,

> If you confess with your mouth Jesus as Lord, and believe in your heart that God raised Him from the dead, you will be saved; for with the heart a person believes, resulting in righteousness, and with the mouth he confesses, resulting in salvation.

Say it. Mean it. *Zing!* The sword goes into the devil and he has to get out of your life. Begin to proclaim the call of God and His purposes in your life as you understand them. And just as God works to transform your life under your new calling, He will soon use you as a means of declaring His purposes over your city. A recent outcome of the cumulative cry of the Church in St. Petersburg: The city was just named as one of the top 26 most liveable cities in America. St. Pete has gone from a city known for its racial division and animosity to a top 26 city to live in.

One way He may lead you to do this is by praying His blessing over your city. The Rev. Ed Silvoso of Harvest Evangelism Ministries encourages people to pronounce God's blessings over their neighbors. Rather than seeing them as "that drunk" or "that heathen" down the street, begin to see them through God's eyes. Try to envision them fulfilling God's purposes for their lives and pray accordingly. You may pray, for example, that a father will become more loving to his children or more faithful and supportive to his wife or that he may prosper at his work. What you are doing is praying God's heavenly will to take place in these individual lives, and by doing so you are indirectly praying God's purposes into your city. As each individual finds and fulfills God's purpose for him or her, he or she will be a part of helping the church in that city herald a new message and fulfill its destiny. Just as you pray God's blessing over people, do the same over your city. Do the same over the congregations of that city.

The El Paso Message

Ehud, as God's leader, was given a specific strategy to follow. As the enemy manifests himself differently in different communities, various strategies arise to proclaim new messages for those cities.

This is the case in El Paso. About 75 pastors are active in a group called "Pastors for Jesus" that began more than a decade ago. Different churches host a two-hour "working luncheon" each month. Their mission is "to unite the Body of Christ in El Paso and take actions as directed by Jesus."

At one meeting they invited civic leaders to come and explore the question, How can we be partners in serving El Paso? Since El Paso has the most teen pregnancies and gangs per capita in the nation, they were led to develop a city-wide charter-education program as a result of that meeting.

And to strengthen marriages and radically reduce divorces in El Paso, these leaders have incorporated a comprehensive program called "Marriage Savers." The goal is to reduce El Paso's four thousand divorces per year to fewer than two thousand per year within the next five years. Mike and Harriet McManus, the national founders of Marriage Savers, are assisting El Paso in this effort.

And most important, since it was estimated that fewer than 20 percent of El Paso residents have read the entire New Testament, Pastors for Jesus voted unanimously to proclaim a "Year of the Bible." About six hundred thousand people received copies of the New Testament and were encouraged to read them through in a year—something that could be accomplished by reading only five minutes a day! The *El Paso Times* agreed to print the daily reading in the newspaper. Among other things, church members handed out Bible bookmarks, listing the daily readings, as well as free Bibles, and participating pastors preached through the New Testament that year.

Barney Field, executive director of Pastors for Jesus, reports that as the Body of Christ in El Paso unites, encouraging progress is being made toward winning El Paso for Jesus.

98

In San Bernardino, California, Somebody Cares Southland implemented a compassion strategy for a serious problem. Forty-five percent of the residents there are on some form of government assistance. The executive director of Somebody Cares has brought churches and ministries together to help meet the physical needs of people by distributing more than five million pounds of food to the community.

I mentioned earlier our prayer evangelism strategy called the Year of Answered Prayer. Church members adopt geographical areas we call "prayer squares." Residents within those squares are targeted with prayer. Businesses within the adopted squares have prayer boxes put in them, and the owners or managers are prayed for along with their businesses. We put up twenty billboards, churches displayed banners, church members placed signs in front of their homes and bumper stickers went on the cars, all announcing The Year of Answered Prayer and simply asking the question, "Need prayer?"

Area pastors began the first two years of this campaign with forty days of prayer and fasting. As a "God consciousness" was raised in Tampa Bay, souls were being added to His Kingdom. Thirty calls a day came in from the billboards. People driving by homes with yard signs literally stopped their cars and went up to the home, asking, "Is this really a house of prayer? My family is a wreck. I need prayer."

> It's a simple question:
>
> Need prayer?

The Lord gave us a strategy to break down the pastors' prayer meetings into smaller zones. Many pastors did not have a vision for their own community—let alone all of Tampa Bay. As the pastors' groups came together in their own areas, they understood that they were a part of something larger, the greater Tampa Bay community. As God would have it, when the Billy Graham Crusade came to Tampa Bay, the planners asked us to use our meetings and the strategic network of prayer they represented to help prepare the area for the crusade.

Another initiative was developed simultaneously with our prayer evangelism strategy: to bridge the racial divide and diffuse the enemy's schemes in this area. The devil is always raising his ugly head when it comes to race. Two pastors in Tampa, Don Evans of Gateway Christian Center and Abe Brown of First Baptist Church of College Hill, rallied the church pastors in the effort. More than four thousand pastors and church members filled the Sundome on the campus of the University of South Florida for a reconciliation event called "Restoration." Their purpose was to commit to being His multicultural, racial, denominational and lingual bouquet of believers. Racial walls began to come down. Later, Restoration joined with Somebody Cares Tampa Bay to put practical restoration into practice. Rather than holding more restoration events, we decided to demonstrate restoration. In partnership with Operation Blessing, we began to come alongside inner-city ministries and help them in practical ways.

God will equip you with His message. Notice that in each case, regardless of the emerging message or strategy, the result is God's people coming together in agreement. The church must agree with the message collectively to reach your community's destiny. As you move forward, certain methods or marching orders will spring forth as well. Various initiatives may even arise with the same objective. It will take humility and love to make sure these initiatives do not clash but, rather, combine as would two or more streams to form a powerful river of God's love flowing in your community. One way to ensure this is by holding core values that will guide the action of the Kingdom-driven church. Core values act as the substance of the message. They underscore that we mean what we say and that we are serious about carrying out the message of God to see His Kingdom fully established in our community.

The next several chapters will depart from the story in Judges 3 to focus on some other key elements. We will conclude with the triumph of Ehud (Union) over the city of Jericho.

9

The Kingdom-Driven Church

The six core values you will be reading about in this chapter are key to seeing God's Kingdom fully established in your area. These values are reflected in heart attitudes that dictate our action. These or similar values must be a part of the framework to achieve the goal of manifesting Christ's presence throughout your entire community. These values provide wisdom so the Church can work smarter not harder, because the job itself is hard enough. Where methods and strategies change, these principles will help us prevail for the long haul.

Seeing our members grow spiritually and the congregation numerically are objectives that do not need to be sacrificed to be a Kingdom-driven church. In fact, the health that God is blessing you with, He wants you to share with others.

Think about all the health pills, diets and exercise machines that we are bombarded to try. Many are gimmicky quick fixes, but others are authentic and can help. If we pick one, it is usually because someone we know and trust lost weight and it did not kill him or her in the process. In the same way your church and other churches in your community have different strengths and weaknesses. God has given us different insights and ways of doing things that have given us success in one way or another. Out of a desire to promote Kingdom growth by building healthy congregations in our community, we should gladly let others know what is working for us. It might not fit every congregation, but it could help someone. The point is that you are fulfilling a greater purpose than just your agenda—the rapid expansion of Christ's Kingdom.

Healthy congregations that are not interested in helping struggling churches can be likened to a bodybuilder named Joe. Joe has a great physique. He makes women swoon and men jealous. Many have asked his secret but Joe refuses to divulge it. Keeping other men in the dark about health and exercise—and in flabby physical condition—makes him look all the better. Joe sounds selfish, prideful and a little insecure.

> **The Kingdom-driven church sees itself as a distinct congregation of believers who belong to a greater Church, whose purpose is to establish the Kingdom of God firmly in its city or community.**

In reality, people with good bodies sell their secrets and resources to help others achieve the same results. In similar fashion we should be willing to share insights and resources so others can achieve our results. Our rewards ultimately are heavenly ones.

Here is a list of our core values at Somebody Cares Tampa Bay. I believe this list could be adopted and added to by any congregation that wants to be a Kingdom-driven church. The Kingdom-driven church sees itself as a distinct congregation of believers who belong to a greater Church, whose purpose is to establish the Kingdom of God firmly in its city or community.

Value 1: Empower Others to Be Bigger, Be Better and Go Farther

A practical way to empower others to be bigger and better and go farther is by a suburban church being a resource to an inner-city congregation. We have done several large distributions of publications such as the *Fallen but Not Forgotten* booklet. This booklet was created by Campus Crusade and gave churches an opportunity to respond to the community after the September 11 attacks. Larger congregations paid for the booklets so smaller Hispanic churches could reach the Hispanic community.

Another example I observed was through the Vineyard Church in Cincinnati. The founding pastor, Steve Sjogren, along with fifty other churches planned a "Serve Cincinnati Day." To show God's love in a practical way, they gave out a hundred thousand cold drinks on a hot June day on street corners throughout the city. The drinks were given to pedestrians walking the sidewalks and to passengers in cars when stopped at red lights at intersections. The Vineyard Church funded the majority of the project. With the drinks they gave what are called "connect cards" telling the recipients that this was a way of showing them God's love. On the other side of the card was the local church's information. The Vineyard Church printed the cards with the other fifty churches' information on it, not their own. They fielded the majority of volunteers. They did this for the other congregations because they are a Kingdom-driven church. This is an example of the role the healthy mega-church plays in reaching its city.

Value 2: What We Cannot Do Apart, We Can Do Together

What the churches have accomplished together in Tampa Bay is something we were largely unable to do apart. We have collectively distributed five hundred thousand *Books of Hope*, annually give away more than fifteen thousand backpacks filled with school supplies and hold a Raise the Roof grassroots evangelistic concert, attended by more than sixteen thousand people.

Another example of cooperative effort is what several small churches did in Dunedin, a town in the Tampa Bay area. Each had done its own back-to-school outreach, but they decided to combine their efforts. For some time they had been praying that the spring training facility used by the Toronto Blue Jays would become available so they could conduct an outreach to their community. I received a phone call from the Blue Jays' organization, a contact that came without any prompting. They wanted to make their stadium available to the local church to host a community event. It was an obvious answer to prayer. The churches worked together in perfect harmony, which was a great witness to the Blue Jays' front office. Nearly one thousand backpacks were given away to needy children. Most heard the Gospel presented, many received prayer, several were saved, but everyone knew the Church was there to serve and to bless.

Value 3: Unity Is Not Optional

I have discussed this in depth but will add this illustration to make the point again. Shoemakers in the Philippines made what they claim are the world's biggest pair of shoes. The shoes, men's size 753, are 18 feet long and 7 feet wide. Thirty shoemakers stood inside the shoe for a picture after it was made. The shoes took 77 days to construct and used $13,135 worth of materials.

Every generation since the ascension of our Lord Jesus has had big shoes to fill—that of being the Body of Christ on earth. And the only way these shoes can be filled to have a worldwide effect is if we work together.

Value 4: Every Part Is Essential to the Greater Whole

No one is too big and no one is too small. My friend Doug Stringer would often introduce a buddy of his, Bubba Chambers, by saying, "Here is Bubba Chambers, president of 'Winning the Whole World All by Myself Ministries.'" Doug would always get a good chuckle. No one congregation is going to win a city all by itself. Granted, larger churches have a major role to play. They have been given greater responsibility in the Kingdom. Yet they must recognize that establishing the Kingdom to its fullest extent in our cities is bigger than they are. They need other congregations and other congregations need them.

While visiting the Star of the Republic Museum in Brazos, Texas, I read a passage from the journal of James Wilson Nichols, a soldier who had been engaged in the struggle for a free Texas. He wrote, "We are few in numbers and the very nature of our situation . . . makes every man a soldier." The battle we are waging is the greatest of all mankind. In every community it is bigger than any one of us and needs all of us. If we are to achieve deliverance and liberty for those enslaved in our cities by the enemy, everyone must become a soldier.

> "We are few in numbers and the very nature of our situation . . . makes every man a soldier."

One evening in June 1945, one hundred thousand people gathered in the Los Angeles Coliseum. They had come together to honor the men from their city who had died in World War II. A mock battle demonstrated the helplessness of the individual. An uneasy silence filled the great coliseum. Then the master of ceremonies spoke: "Perhaps you sometimes say to yourself, 'My job isn't important because it's such a little job.' But you are wrong. The most obscure person can be very important. Let me show you what I mean."

105

He ordered the lights turned off. There was total darkness. Then he struck a match and, in the darkness, the one flickering light could be seen by the multitude.

"Now you can see the importance of one little light," he said. "Suppose we all strike a light."

Suddenly across the vast stadium, thousands of pinpoints of light brightened the summer night. The darkness had first been penetrated by one little light and then followed by thousands.

You are important. The world will be a little better or worse because of you. You really count.

You are needed. You cannot do everything, but you can do something.

Jesus said, "Look at the birds of the air, that they do not sow, nor reap nor gather into barns, and yet your heavenly Father feeds them. Are you not worth much more than they?" (Matthew 6:26). The Lord is saying that small is beautiful.

**Value 5: Support What God Has Already Established,
Rather than Duplicating or Recreating**

This is especially true regarding compassion ministries. We publish an annual resource directory of Christ-centered compassion ministries. It gives churches an awareness of the various ministries and what needs they are meeting.

If people call your church with particular needs you are not equipped to meet, you can turn to someone who is. It also helps a pastor to know that, rather than starting his own soup kitchen, there is one down the road his church can assist.

Our Carefest—A Week of Caring does the same thing. Compassion ministries submit projects that volunteers will be able to do in a three-to-four-hour period. Churches and businesses can get a small taste of doing compassion outreach, through a ministry they never before had a relationship with. The ministry gets a positive jolt, with potentially ongoing help. The church gets a member with a renewed vision and passion to reach others.

Smaller churches need to recognize that they are significant and cannot be uninvolved. I have had pastors of large congregations tell me they are concerned that their involvement will run other pastors off. Others may fear that the big church pastor has come to take over. We all need to come to the table acknowledging that each has a contribution. We must serve one another because we need each other. The job is bigger than any one of us.

Value 6: Mobilization Is the Key to a Sustained Spiritual Awakening and Transformation of Our Communities

Long before T. D. Jakes preached and wrote, "Woman, Thou Art Loosed," Jesus said it. Jesus loosed His Bride, the Church, more than two thousand years ago with all the authority given Him, with what we know as the Great Commission, "Go therefore and make disciples of all the nations" (Matthew 28:19).

This is where we truly need to have a vision of something bigger than ourselves. This may mean releasing people to ministry that may not be directly connected to your church. How do you change the spiritual climate in your community? Most cities are smaller communities that make up the larger. Affecting one of those positively can only help the others.

A large Christian center in Tampa had not had much success canvassing neighborhoods with literature. When it came to passing out one hundred thousand care packages door to door to kick off Carefest week, they were not interested. A smaller church, which was attempting to reach a depressed area in the city, was. The larger church decided

107

to come alongside and help the smaller church deliver care packages.

I believe a simple strategy for transformation is this: Put light into darkness. The more light you put in the darkness, the less darkness there will be. The more we can create avenues where people can shine their lights, the better we will be. It may not have an immediate impact on the numbers being added to your congregation, but it will create laborers rather than lazy, unproductive members.

> **Put light into darkness. The more light you put in the darkness, the less darkness there will be.**

We add spiritual vitality to our churches as each person begins to fulfill his or her destiny, using his or her spiritual gifts and talents to touch lives. As we keep actively applying these values, the spiritual climate in our communities will change and the congregations will overflow with new converts. The next several chapters will expand on this last core value—mobilization. First let's focus on mobilizing the marketplace.

10

Marketplace Impact

If we are to be God's gift to our cities, everyone must play a part. Businesspeople comprise a large and influential segment of the Church community that needs to be networked and mobilized. The businessperson is an indispensable part of the Body of Christ in reaching every community. As the following story suggests, most pastors understand this idea.

A small private plane crashed on a deserted island. One survivor asked the other, "How are we going to get off this island?"

The other survivor, a wealthy businessman, said, "I'm not worried. I make a hundred thousand dollars a week."

"Fine," said the first survivor. "But don't you think we should make a fire, try and build a boat or write SOS in the sand?"

The businessman again calmly said, "I'm not worried. I make a hundred thousand dollars a week."

Irritated, the other man said, "How is your hundred thousand dollars a week going to get you off this island?"

He replied, "I make a hundred thousand dollars a week and I give ten percent of it to my church. I am confident that my pastor is going to find me."

Here is another insightful story illustrating the power and influence a businessman, anointed by God, can have on a city. Businessman Brian Taylor took steps in church unity to help reach his city of Aberdeen, Scotland. Though his company was small, he sought to reach out to the poor and needy. He decided, "If no one else is going to do it on a city-wide basis, then I will." In less than six months, with the help of those local churches in agreement, he procured and distributed 350 tons of food into the city.

They are now distributing furniture and have a clothing warehouse with new clothes. They built the second-largest skating park in Scotland, but because of local-government opposition they had to close it. Then, as people prayed, the Lord moved. The labor administration that was opposed to the skating park lost their positions and a new leadership was established. The provost (mayor), the chief executive of the city and the leader of the council are all born-again Christians. The park is now reopened. Brian's business is now a multimillion-dollar enterprise. The proverb has been fulfilled through Brian that says, "He who is generous will be blessed, for he gives some of his food to the poor" (Proverbs 22:9).

The importance of the person in the marketplace is not new. Businesspeople played an important role in establishing the first-century Church. Jesus was involved in the family business. He learned the carpenter's trade from His earthly father, Joseph. His disciples were from the business community as well—fishermen, a tax collector, etc. Dr. Luke was an asset to Paul's ministry. Aquila and Priscilla made tents. Dorcas, a seamstress, was raised from the dead. Peter stayed in Joppa with a tanner named Simon. Lydia of Thyatira was a merchant of purple garments and responded to Paul's message of the Gospel. There are many other business people mentioned in Scripture.

The business community has been instrumental in establishing a new paradigm for the present-day church. And that is to see the big "C" Church in a community come together to have the impact God intended for it to have. Businesspeople have been a vital part of assisting Somebody Cares Tampa Bay. As I began sharing the vision of mobilizing Christians as a caring community to transform Tampa Bay, they quickly gravitated to it. Businesspeople, whether they own or manage a company, want to reach their communities.

> **Businesses played an important role in the early Church.**

Businesspeople: Assets for Reaching Your City

Let me share some insights about Christian businesspeople that have helped me understand and motivate them to be involved in city-wide efforts.

- They want to be known as community-minded, both personally and as a business.
- They have faith and are willing to take risks to be in business. They understand stepping out in faith, taking risks to do a God-sized thing in the community.
- Business people believe that they are called to their geographical areas and to their particular businesses. They believe, therefore, that they are God-ordained to be His minister in the marketplace, just as a pastor or ministry leader feels called to a church.
- Many see their businesses as God's vehicle for ministry to establish the Kingdom of God to its fullest. Businesspeople want to do more than go to church on Sundays and Wednesdays and pay their tithes. They want to be part of something bigger than themselves.

111

Whenever I gather businesspeople together and share these principles, you can see heads nodding in agreement, as if lights are coming on.

A great booklet that helps impart this Kingdom mindset and that explains how business leaders and those in ministry work together is *Kings and Priests* by David R. Hightower.

The business community sponsors our annual Raise the Roof evangelistic concert; about two thousand underprivileged children attend this event. They provide the resources for our annual compassion banquet, where we honor local ministries for their often thankless work among the disadvantaged. We find that at least one-third of the volunteers for Carefest—A Week of Caring are business owners and their employees.

> **The Christian business community is the best day-to-day witness the Church has in its community.**

Those in the business community offer resources, finances and wisdom to the Body. But they are more than that. They are also the best day-to-day witnesses the Church can have in a community. They are in contact with the unreached community every day, meeting people that the clergy will never encounter. Plus the unsaved can identify more readily with them. They are in the real "dog-eat-dog" world and are maintaining their Christian values and commitment.

Buck Jacobs is the founder of C12, a ministry that mentors CEOs. They emphasize doing business with excellence and as a believer in Christ. Each CEO is responsible for personal ministry, ministry to his or her employees and ministry to his or her community. Buck shared his commitment to this end in one of his monthly messages entitled, "Your Business as a Vehicle for Ministry." Among other things, he said:

> Our business is a vehicle or platform for bringing forth or applying the "good news." A vehicle is something that we

use to take us somewhere or that we utilize to some end. And a platform is a foundation or basis for action or a support for something.[1]

Buck's thoughts are based on personal experience. Here is one instance where his business gave him a platform for a successful witnessing opportunity that he would not have had otherwise.

One evening several years ago, Buck was settling back in his seat on a flight from somewhere in the south, going to Chicago. Buck was dog-tired. After a long, rough week all he wanted to do was to read the *Wall Street Journal* long enough to put himself to sleep.

As he was opening the paper he noticed the woman seated next to him smiling a sort of timid smile in his direction. Buck quickly looked away, not wanting to talk to her.

She spoke first, "Are you going home?"

"Yes," he answered, not wanting to say more.

"I'm not," she said. "I'm visiting my son and new grand-baby."

"That's nice."

"What do you do?" At this point he knew his plan for sleep was on hold. Buck had learned that when people asked him this question he was to respond in a specific way.

"I work for a very unusual company," he said. "It's a chemical business that's a Christian company."

"How unusual!" she replied.

Realizing now that his plans for sleep were not going to happen, Buck responded, "Yes, it is unusual. We are trying to learn and to show how Jesus would run a business if He were the boss." He looked at her intently. *Sweet-looking little old lady*, Buck thought. *I wonder what the Lord has in store through this divine appointment?*

"I haven't been to church for many years. I just didn't get anything from it," she said.

"I never got much from church either, not until I met Jesus and gave my life to Him. It's different now," Buck replied.

You may know the rest. Maxine Smith of Greenville, Tennessee, had been to church many times but had never met the Lord of the Church. Not until that night. That night she became Buck's friend and sister in Christ.

She went home and shared what had happened with her husband. They started to go to church and joy entered and filled their lives. She wrote to Buck for many years, blessing him with stories of how the Lord was using her. Buck would read the letters in his Sunday school class, and everyone would learn much from Maxine. She had some hard times. But when the Lord got her heart, He got all of it!

In telling this story to his C12 members, Buck said: "If it hadn't been for the business, I wouldn't have been on that plane at all. And if I hadn't been there, might God have used someone else? Perhaps. But the point is, He didn't. He used me because He put me in the business and sent me there. The business was the reason I was on the plane."

My objective is to give these businesses tools to facilitate their witnessing opportunities in the marketplace. We already mentioned the prayer boxes. The majority of those six hundred boxes were placed in businesses. We encouraged those who became a part of our "Business Professionals Who Care" group to add these words to their business cards: "I'm a business professional who cares! Need prayer?" We found that most people will not turn down a compassionate appeal to pray for them.

Bart Azzarelli, who heads a local construction company, puts his bold mission statement on his business card, letterhead and on the construction site. His mission statement is: "The purpose of our business is to glorify God by serving you with the most excellent product possible, that by this our Lord Jesus might be able to say, 'Well done, good and faithful servant.'"

114

Here are 56 ways your business can be a vehicle for ministry.

1. Take this book and implement it. Share its principles with another business owner.
2. Put a prayer box in your business so employees and patrons can submit requests and be prayed for. Encourage other businesses to do the same.
3. Be a business of hope. Pray for your immediate marketplace. (For those other businesses around you, too!)
4. Have a compassion-resource directory or helpline directory in your office to guide those you come in contact with who may need directions in getting help.
5. Have a teddy bear drive. Have employees bring in teddy bears for local police to give to children victimized by domestic violence.
6. Adopt a cop. Adopt your local law enforcement and their families and do something special for them.
7. Prepare a mission statement that identifies you as a Christian business with a ministry objective. Put it on your business card.
8. Have a chaplain for your employees, a local pastor or ministry leader who will be available once a week. Contact Corporate Chaplains of America online at: http://www.iamchap.org
9. Establish a weekly prayer time and Bible study before or after hours or during the lunch break for those interested.
10. Dedicate your business to God. Have a dedication service.
11. Have an apprenticeship program so young adults/teens can learn about your business and develop professional skills.
12. Hire disadvantaged people who have gone through a life-skills course and need employment.

13. Commit to giving liberally from the business to help promote the Gospel in your city.
14. Provide services to local pastors and other full-time Christian leaders for a big discount or free (for example, a free website or website maintenance).
15. Lend your employees to a local ministry that needs administrative help.
16. Conduct a drive for baby items for local pregnancy centers. Throw a baby shower for one of the women committed to keeping her baby.
17. Do a tennis-shoe drive to provide shoes for the homeless.
18. Include a small gift item, candy, gum, etc. when you bill your customers or when you pay your bills to show God's love. Items such as Testamints and other creative candies can be found in most Christian bookstores.
19. Pay for your employees to go see a Christian concert or "Success in Life" seminar.
20. Take a day and serve at a local soup kitchen.
21. Wash windows for other businesses located near your business.
22. Wash cars for other businesses located near your business.
23. Take out the trash for other businesses located near your business.
24. Clean the bathrooms for other businesses located near your business.
25. Host a luncheon on Boss' Day for the different bosses in your marketplace.
26. Host a luncheon on Secretaries' Day so other bosses can show their appreciation.
27. Share the resumes of good Christian employees you may not be able to hire with other companies. The idea is to have these Christian employees understand that God is placing them to be a witness.
28. Bless your competitor.

29. When giving out paychecks, write a note of appreciation for the good week(s) employees have put in.
30. Provide a financial management seminar for your employees and others so they can stay out of debt and use their money wisely. They will see these principles coming from God's Word.
31. Make a list of the names of family members of your employees, their ages and birthdays, anniversaries, etc. Send a note to them on their special days and possibly a gift. Encourage fellow employees to remember each other.
32. Conduct a Carefest week. Each day is a different day of caring.
33. Make up business cards saying: A Business Who Cares—Need Prayer?
34. Locate a marriage seminar and pay for employees to go to it.
35. Get with other businesses and put on an appreciation banquet for the various compassion ministries in your community.
36. When a customer has paid his bill in full, send an invoice with a little note that says, "Good news—You are 'paid in full.' Those were the words Jesus spoke when He hung on the cross for your sins."
37. Incorporate an exchange policy. Those in retail business can put up a sign that reads: "Ask about our exchange policy." When a customer asks, let her know about the actual policy you may have, and then ask if she would like to hear about the best exchange policy on the planet—how Christ has exchanged our righteousness, which is as filthy rags, and has clothed us in His righteousness.
38. List Jesus Christ as the owner of your business and you as steward on your letterhead.
39. Take an employee out to lunch, just to get to know him or her better.

40. Develop a hit list. Have the Bible study group compile a top-ten list of people to pray for. These people can be those receptive or close to coming to Christ.
41. Give out "care" coupons.
42. Dress for success. Provide dress clothes from quality thrift stores (suits, dresses, shoes) for those who do not have the means to buy them for job interviews.
43. Donate computers to after-school programs. Donate your time to children in the programs to teach computer skills.
44. Pay your employees to be involved with a community outreach, Habitat for Humanity, Somebody Cares Day or similar event or activity.
45. Pay someone's electric bill or rent. Have an emergency fund to help those in need.
46. Provide a car giveaway or repair. Work with other businesses to help single moms get their cars repaired or actually get a car. Unemployment or lower-paying jobs are often due to a lack of mobility.
47. Overpay your bill.
48. Teach seniors how to be computer literate. In exchange ask them to mentor youth or volunteer for small ministries that need help.
49. Send emails to missionaries overseas to encourage them.
50. Collect hats for cancer patients who lose their hair.
51. Prepare several ways to answer the question, "What do you do for a living?" Refer to Buck Jacobs' testimony on the plane.
52. Host a lunch for local pastors in the area.
53. Work with the local Christian chiropractors to put on Kid's Day America, a national outreach to kids conducted by chiropractors across the country (check their website).
54. Write out a salvation and business testimony that simply tells others how God has blessed your life.

55. Provide a babysitter so a single mom who works for you can go out. Buy a movie ticket and dinner for her and a friend or offer to take her out with your spouse.
56. Give away free stuff (bottled water, cold soda). Along with the free stuff, give a care card that explains why you are doing it (see our website for samples).

The mobilized marketplace helps put the haves with the have-nots. A business, when mobilized, often ends up in a great marriage with compassion ministries who are transforming lives in the city. In the next chapter we will look at why compassion is not only a key to opening our cities to Jesus, it is a main component for long-term transformation.

II

Compassion—the Key to City Impact

After ballooning to 232 pounds, I decided it was time to lose some weight. I began running three miles several days a week and, in a year, had lost thirty pounds. But in spite of the weight loss, my body shape did not change. Dissatisfied with the results, I began the popular "Body for Life" program by Bill Phillips. In his book, also titled *Body for Life*, he notes several myths and facts. Here is one myth: Aerobics are better for shaping up than weight training. Here is the fact: To transform your physique, you must train with weights.[1]

There is a parallel to seeing the Body of Christ and our cities transformed. Myth: Sufficient corporate prayer alone will transform your congregation and the church in your city. Fact: To transform your congregation and the Body of Christ in your city, prayer must be complemented with the exercise of the many gifts, especially that of compassion, service and evangelism. The spiritual Body of Christ also has different parts and gifts that must be exercised to reach optimum health and, through that health, we can transform a city. In this chapter we will look at how mobilizing the Church in the area of compassion plays an essential role in bringing about and sustaining transformation in your community.

Compassion Will Sustain Transformation

Presence evangelism is sometimes described as the presence of Jesus being manifested in a city as we pray. I agree that through concentrated, united prayer Christ's manifest presence can be felt in a tangible way in the community. The Welsh Revivals, that of New York through revivalist Charles Finney and others, have shown that through concentrated, united prayer Christ's presence has been manifested in a tangible way in communities. But to sustain His presence and to see transformation take place, we need to mobilize the Body in a myriad of practical ways. Presence evangelism occurs when a believer is equipped with the presence of God, through the indwelling of the Holy Spirit, and is mobilized in the community. Because the Spirit of Christ indwells the believer, so Christ is there as well. As we do deeds of kindness, compassion and other service we are shining our lights so others will see our good deeds and praise our Father who is in heaven.

Aerobics are a cardiovascular workout. In other words they condition your heart. Other exercise methods, such as weight training, condition and transform the body using other muscles. Prayer is the spiritual equivalent of aerobics. It conditions your heart. Your heart becomes in tune with God and more compassionate to those around you. Yet prayer must be combined with the exercise of other gifts in the Body of Christ if a city or a church in the city is going to be transformed.

122

An area where the church can exercise many of its gifts like mercy, service, hospitality, evangelism and intercession is compassion. If prayer is the key to heaven, then compassion is the key to our cities. In the past the church has generally thrown away the key to the city by neglecting the needy.

It is not a recent problem. Mark 6:33–36 records the feeding of the five thousand, saying:

> The people saw them [Jesus and the apostles] going, and many recognized them and ran there together on foot from all the cities, and got there ahead of them. When Jesus went ashore, He saw a large crowd, and He felt compassion for them because they were like sheep without a shepherd; and He began to teach them many things. When it was already quite late, His disciples came to Him and said, "This place is desolate and it is already quite late; send them away so that they may go into the surrounding countryside and villages and buy themselves something to eat."

The disciples' first reaction to the physical needs of the multitude is, "Lord, send them away." They are willing to send them away before knowing their capacity to meet the need. Jesus asks them, "How many loaves do you have? Go look." How do you know you can't feed them? Go check your resources is what Jesus was saying. The disciples did not want to meet the multitude's needs out of their own resources.

> The key to heaven is prayer. The key to our cities is compassion.

At this point in the ministry of Jesus, it was entertaining to follow Him. You got great teaching and miracles. By hanging out with Jesus to watch Him perform, you could have deluded yourself into thinking that you were a true follower.

Not much has changed in two thousand years. We have great Christian entertainment, movies, concerts and speakers easily available. We do all we can to be entertaining on

123

Sunday at church. People could delude themselves today into believing that they are true followers because they hang out at church or enjoy Christian entertainment. But when it comes to serving and meeting needs of others, such "believers" find it easier to send them away.

Excuses Have Not Changed

After discovering their resources, just five loaves and two fish (see Mark 6:38), the disciples have a legitimate reason to send the crowds away. The resources-to-need ratio is not very good. The five thousand gathered there counts only men. When you add women and children, the ranks of the hungry number around ten thousand people. To give the disciples credit, they have a good excuse based on reason. But God's works can never be done according to human standards and reasoning. When we attempt to do so, they cease to be God's work and become man's work.

The resources-to-need ratio has not gotten much better. The needs in American cities and other countries are on the rise. We, as the Church, have adopted human reasoning like the disciples before us to "send them away." Here are a few of our excuses:

1. "There are too many." The number of poor, especially working poor, is great and increasing daily. But this does not get us off the hook. We can get overwhelmed by the need. God has called us to do what we can where we are.
2. "It is going to require too much." This seems to be the cry of the disciples. "Shall we go spend two hundred denarii on bread to give them something to eat?" They were saying, "Jesus, are You asking us to spend our own money to feed these people?" The undertone sounds like, "Jesus, You are asking too much."

124

3. "The return on our investment will be too little." The church wants "bang for its buck." If I spend money, I want to see a return on my investment, like more people in the pews or dollars in the offering.

4. "It is dangerous." It can be. My wife and I took into our home men who were ex-cons and drug addicts trying to kick their dependency and we rented and moved into another house across the street. One night I asked the men, "How do you know Jesus has changed your life?"

Martin, a young Hispanic man, replied, "I know God is changing me because I haven't stolen anything from you yet." I thought to myself, *Time to hide the keys, honey.* Let me add, we always need to take proper precautions. But the point is, there is danger in our world and danger in doing God's will. The question is not, Is it dangerous? The question is, Is it God's will?

5. "I will be taken advantage of." Without a doubt you will be taken advantage of, just as Christ healed and helped many only to see some of them join the mob that called for His crucifixion.

6. "We pay taxes for government programs to take care of them." Government programs have a legitimate use. We need to partner with the government as a resource, complementing our efforts. Government help does not allow us to abandon Christ's call on His Church to care for the needy.

7. "Let's send them to a para-church organization that is set up better to meet their needs." The church needs to join with other ministries and other ministries need to join with the church.

8. "I would do it, but I don't know how." This is not a good excuse. I believe that if you have the heart, God will show you the how. I did not know how to do street ministry. God put it on my heart, and my

wife and I went into the projects, feeding and teaching people as God led.

After several years of consistent outreach, our work gained a good reputation in the twin towns of Bryan/College Station, Texas. A friend, who pastored a large Methodist church, asked me to come preach and then teach for six weeks on how to care for the poor. I had to stop and ask myself, How do you do this? The answer is really no different from caring for your neighbor. Get to know them and care for them. Ask God to provide beyond your simple means.

We have used all the above excuses and more to send the needy away. In fact the church has sent them away for years. As we send the needy away, our credibility as true followers goes with them. As we send them away, we are throwing away the keys to our cities' and churches' destinies in every community.

In previous chapters we have looked at how the cities that make up Tampa Bay have opened to our ministry. On one occasion, when President George W. Bush was to visit Tampa, the mayor's office was asked to pick a ministry that best demonstrated the goals of the president's faith-based initiative. The officials said the first name that came to their minds was Somebody Cares Tampa Bay. Compassion brings back credibility to the church. It opens the city.

In a nutshell the disciples' excuses went like this, "We don't have enough money; there is not enough food on hand; even if we did have enough food, there are so many people that it would be a logistical nightmare to feed them. Besides, it's late and we are tired. Send them away!"

And Jesus says, "Yeah, you're right. How foolish of Me! They've made it thus far; they can fend for themselves one more day. Send them away."

Wrong! Jesus turns to the disciples and says, "You give them something to eat!"(verse 37). In other words, the people do not need to go away. *You* feed them. Jesus is testing the disciples' compassion and commitment. Jesus does not say that they are supposed to supply the food. He says, "You commit to feeding them and I will supply."

In Luke's gospel (9:18–22), immediately following the feeding Jesus asks the disciples, "Who do the people say that I am?"

They answer, "John the Baptist, and others say Elijah; but others, that one of the prophets of old has risen again."

"Who do you say that I am?" Jesus questions the disciples.

Peter says, "The Christ of God."

Then Jesus proceeds to tell them how He will suffer, die and rise again.

Jesus could have "taken care of business" Himself. He could have sat them down and called on the Father to send food from heaven. Instead He gives the disciples a challenge and a thought-provoking exercise. He wants them to realize who He is and what He can do. He wants them to understand who is among them: The Christ, the Son of God.

This incident is part of the disciples' compassion training. Jesus is going away soon. These hungry followers are going to become the responsibility of the disciples. Jesus is trying to teach them how to depend on Him to meet the needs of their future flock. In essence Jesus is saying, "These people are soon going to be your sheep, your responsibility—you feed them." They are learning how to depend on Jesus to care for His sheep.

Shepherding the City Is Physical and Spiritual

I have heard pastors' groups say that they are the shepherds of the city: They shepherd it collectively. I believe that is correct. Shepherding a city means we lean on Jesus collectively to meet the needs of the hungry and disadvantaged in our community. As we commit collectively to shepherding all peoples of our city, God will supernaturally supply. The experience of Bishop Bart Pierce and the Rock Church in Baltimore, Maryland, are a case in point as they committed to meet the needs of the disadvantaged in their community. Here is his testimony.

Compassion has been a powerful vehicle to open the favor of God on our ministry here in Baltimore. We moved here in 1983 and have seen tremendous favor since the first week. Because we stepped into every jail and prison ministry in our city, we have been asked to work with every penal system. The courts assign people to our men's shelter, Nehemiah House, and our girl's home, The Hiding Place. If a judge knows that the individual before him or her is working through one of our programs, he or she will set a court order that they must stay with our program.

We now have a "first of a kind" direct website feed from our church website into the prison. It allows the inmates to view our services, special programs that we develop just for the prisoners and other programs that we choose. It is set up so that they can go only to our website and nowhere else. We also wrote the prison manual for the religious activities. Our prison director is now chairing a new program with the mayor and the wardens that will reach the paroled as they are released.

Because we have been feeding thousands of people through our "A Can Can Make a Difference" program each year, we have again seen the favor of the Lord. We move more than a million pounds of food through our city each year. When the Word of God says "if we are a friend to the poor, God makes us His friend," it is true! We have been given two huge warehouses that are forty thousand square feet each. In addition we have three tractor-trailers, forklifts and all kinds of equipment that help make our food ministry flourish. Because we have always given our food away free, many businesses and leaders are attracted to our ministry.

A number of major companies work with us, such as: Hard Rock Café, Chick-fil-A, Unilever, Maryland Transit

Authority and Fila. Many others have joined us in our efforts to feed the poor and their contributions help us to be very successful. From the mayor's office to the police department, to the many social programs in our city and even to the residences and churches, there is one clear message: A Can Can Make a Difference. Whenever we need city assistance, the city, the Oriole's baseball park, and the churches have been touched and moved upon to work together because of our compassionate lead.

When it comes to working with the growing problem of homelessness and drug and substance dependency, the governor, the city and our counties know that the number-one program they have come to depend on to change men's lives is the Nehemiah House. With a 71 percent success rate, it is a very structured and excellently run program that takes men from every level and transforms them into productive citizens. Fine Christian men, with families and new jobs, are being introduced back into society with a mission and a new commitment to be all that God has purposed them to be. More than four thousand men have been through the program since it began, and it continues to grow in number every year. The county gives us millions of dollars each year, and the private sector gives into the program on a regular basis. The state has just given us an additional twelve acres of land to open a new ten-unit transitional housing facility.

Reaching out to the poor defined Jesus as the Christ. It must define you as His follower.

Businessmen in our city have been so moved by what they see happening that they have joined in to help. We have been given twelve houses in the city and are picking up four more in the near future. Our plan is to have one thousand houses given to us to transform into homes suitable for families to live in, and then we will place first-time buyers in them. This will bring great joy to many families whose dream has been to own their own home. These homes are a part of our city transformation program called "Adopt-a-Block."

129

We are taking back whole city blocks in the hopes of seeing our city totally transformed.

These are just a few of the things that God has had us doing for the past twenty years. We believe that, like Joseph of old, we are called to rescue our city and to provoke the church to love and good works. We built our church on a word the Lord spoke to me many years ago while riding through the city. He said, *If you'll take the ones nobody wants, I'll give you the ones everybody is after.* For the church in America to gain credibility as the answer to our cities' needs, we must ask the Lord for His heart for our cities. His heart of compassion for our cities is what will bring a revival transformation to America.

Bishop Pierce understood that the Church needs the inner-city poor more than the inner city needs the Church. In Appendix A, I list "Twenty-seven Reasons Why the Church Needs the Poor." Let me share briefly with you the 27th reason: To define ourselves as true followers of Christ. Reaching out to the poor defined Jesus as the Christ or Messiah. It must define you as His follower.

Reading from Matthew's gospel we find John the Baptist in a dark, dingy prison. He is hearing many different opinions circulating about Jesus. It causes him to question his whole life's purpose. Did he prepare the way for the wrong person? Has he failed God? John sends two of his disciples to ask Jesus, "Are You the Expected One, or shall we look for someone else?" (Matthew 11:3). In today's language, he might have said, "Are you the real deal or should we keep on looking?" Jesus answered:

> "Go and report to John what you hear and see: the blind receive sight and the lame walk, the lepers are cleansed and the deaf hear, the dead are raised up, and the poor have the gospel preached to them."

Matthew 11:4–5

In essence Jesus tells John's disciples that one defining element—just as important as all the miracles that define Him as the Christ—is that the poor are having the Gospel preached to them. The question for you and me is, If preaching the Good News to the poor defined Jesus as the Christ, what should define us as His followers?

As we reflect on our story of the feeding of the five thousand, notice that Jesus first takes care of their logistical problem. Scripture tells us that "He commanded them all to sit down by groups on the green grass. They sat down in groups of hundreds and of fifties" (Mark 6:39–40). He has the disciples break the mob down into small manageable numbers. The task then appears to be less overwhelming and more doable. It is like the answer to the question, "How do you eat an elephant?" "One bite at a time." Jesus broke this elephant-sized project into bite sizes.

We need to do the same with the overwhelming needs in our communities. That is why we developed a compassion-ministries resource directory—so churches can know who is doing what in our community and be able to join in. Ministry becomes more manageable and efforts are not duplicated. By putting this network together to meet the needs of our community, we are preparing for the revival we are praying for. Noah believed that a flood was coming and, on faith, built an ark. Likewise we put together this network, preparing for the rain of God's Spirit that brings the flood of revival.

Ken Ritz, pastor of the Vineyard Church in Hamilton, Ohio, had tried many different ways to bring the churches together. "The only thing that has worked is serving the needy in our community," Ken told me. "Everyone could agree upon meeting the needs of the working poor and disadvantaged." A community ministry called "Serve City" was started. Approximately fifty churches work together. They own a large warehouse that has been totally funded by local foundations and government grants.

Next Jesus broke the bread, blessed it and continued to give it to the disciples until all were fed.

> And He took the five loaves and the two fish, and looking up toward heaven, He blessed the food and broke the loaves and He kept giving them to the disciples to set before them; and He divided up the two fish among them all. They all ate and were satisfied, and they picked up twelve full baskets of the broken pieces, and also of the fish. There were five thousand men who ate the loaves.

> Mark 6:41–44

They had more than enough—twelve baskets full of leftovers. Here Jesus is teaching us Kingdom mathematics. Jesus + resources = more than enough. There was not a supply problem. You might say there was a distribution problem. The homeless coalitions in Tampa Bay reported the need for more food to take care of the growing poverty. Through Operation Blessing we had a way to bring in food trucks. We had enough funds for four trucks for one month. We tried to make a commitment to supply this food at no cost or with as little cost as possible to the compassion ministries and churches.

> **Kingdom mathematics means that there will be more than enough.**

The local TV station picked up the story. The editor from a local newspaper was skeptical. In fact he voiced his opinion that this program would be nonexistent in three months. Three years later (as of this writing), we still have four trucks rolling in. We have brought in more than five million pounds of food, about 150,000 pounds monthly. Approximately ninety churches and ministries are supplied each month. We are shepherding the city even with physical needs. We committed to feeding and God has faithfully supplied.

One of our distribution centers needed a forklift. Chuck Richards, pastor of Kings Avenue Baptist Church, said he knew of a businessman, Roy Jaeger, who might help, which he did. As I called Roy to thank him, he replied, "No, thank you. You have done more for my business than the price of this forklift."

I was surprised at his response, since this was my first communication with him. "How do you mean?" I asked.

"Because of these food trucks and other help, my current office assistant was helped in a time of need. She was going to move out of the area to find work and take care of her family. She was able to stay and work with us. She has been a great asset to my company—so thank you!" he said. This is what happens when you shepherd your city in every way.

As I stated in a previous chapter, I want habitation not visitation. I want Christ to dwell in my community. This means that revival must be sustained. The only way we sustain revival is by mobilizing God's church to be involved in the community. This is presence evangelism—each of us being filled with the Spirit of God and taking Christ's presence into the city.

In Eugene Peterson's paraphrase of the New Testament, *The Message*, John 1:14 states, "The Word became flesh and blood, and moved into the neighborhood." We are now the present incarnation. We are the flesh and blood, inhabited by the Holy Spirit, moving into our neighborhoods and inner cities. Christ is moving into our communities to transform them. As we move into our neighborhoods to care, we become God's gift to our neighbors and, collectively, to our cities.

A close friend of ours, Bev, is a good example of someone caring for her neighborhood. Shortly after Bev and her family moved into their new home, her children were in the front yard playing. Two men, a homosexual couple, who lived across the street came out and began to scold them.

Bev came out when she heard the commotion and asked the men not to yell at her children.

Bev reached out to all the neighbors on her block but had a special burden for the homosexual pair in spite of the bad beginning. She noticed one day that one of the men, Steve (not his real name), was sick, and the Lord told her to take a meal to him. With a prepared meal in hand, she rang the doorbell. But before she could say a word, she heard a voice yell from within, "Go away, we don't want any."

"But I'm—" Bev tried to explain, but the voice kept saying, *"Go away!"*

Dejected, Bev began to walk back across the street when the garage door opened and the healthy partner, Paul (not his real name), came out. He approached her and said, "I'm sorry about the yelling. My partner is dying, and we're stressed out." Bev replied that she just wanted to bring his ailing companion a meal, a Chinese dinner she had prepared. He responded wistfully, "Chinese is his favorite dish."

Not long after, Steve died. And the first place Paul went was to Bev's home for prayer. Time went by and Bev continued to reach out and be friendly until God impressed upon her heart to go share the Gospel with him. Although he did not respond, he knew that someone cared and said he would think about it. Several weeks went by and then there was a knock at her door. There stood Paul. He was visibly upset, having learned that Steve's father had just died. He declared, "I'm ready for Jesus." Bev was able to share her faith with him again and lead him to the Lord.

The moral of this story is that small deeds done with great love can have an impact on even the hardest heart. You can make a difference in your neighborhood and throughout your community.

12

The Power of One

The movie *The Power of One* is a true story about the black African struggle against apartheid in South Africa. At the end of the dramatic movie, this quote appears: "The many can bring change when the many become that which is invincible—the power of one." Let's return now to our story of Ehud.

After killing the king of Moab and returning to the hill country of Ephraim, Ehud blows a trumpet to call the Israelites together. He proclaims: "Pursue them, for the LORD has given your enemies the Moabites into your hands" (Judges 3:28). What a statement of faith! Yes, King Eglon has been slain but that does not necessarily mean the city is theirs for the taking.

Yet Judges 3:29 tells us of the formidable foe they conquer: "They struck down at that time about ten thousand Moabites, all robust and valiant men; and no one escaped." As the passage notes, these were "robust and valiant men," like the Navy Seals or Green Berets of the mighty Moabite army. Remember, for eighteen years this army had intimidated the people of God in Jericho. For nearly two decades, they seemed invincible. And then in one dramatic battle, this same enemy is not only defeated but completely wiped out. What a difference a day can make. How could such a dramatic turnaround take place? The answer is through the power of one.

Ehud Seizes the Moment

Momentum is one of the key elements in war. Ehud seizes the moment when momentum, hope and faith are at their height. I can just hear him saying, "All by my lonesome I entered the king's chamber and slew him. If the hand of the Lord is on one person to kill the king of our enemy, His hand will surely be on all of us as we unite to turn away this oppression and wipe out the enemies of God's city."

I believe we are at the place where the churches in our cities must seize the moment. Most mission-minded leaders, like Dr. Paul Cedar of Mission America, concur that we are on the bubble of the greatest revival America has ever seen.

Jesus really does want to embrace our cities and bring a WOW not a woe. Remember, the definition of WOW is "a work of wonder that is done by the Holy Spirit through Christ's Church." It is doing what we, the Church, can do that the world cannot. It is loving, caring, praying and seeing God and His Kingdom miraculously manifest as we obey the Head, Jesus Christ.

Leaders must proclaim by faith that God's time to reach the city is at hand, but they must demonstrate it by leading. Ehud did not say, "Okay, guys, I have done my part now you do yours. You go down there and take the Moabite army." The Bible records that "the sons of Israel went down with him from the hill country, and he was in front of them" (verse 27).

We must demonstrate our leadership not only by proclaiming God's victory in our cities but also by being out in front as we seek to mobilize God's people. If you are implementing a strategy, you must be out in front, doing so personally.

Unified Mobilization of God's People

We have touched on mobilization extensively in the last two chapters. The second reason the Israelites overcame was that they were mobilized into action. Mobilization of God's people is the key to revival. One of our slogans is "Mobilizing the Whole Body for the Whole Bay."

Jesus tells us in Matthew 9:36–38 that the key to the harvest is more laborers. To paraphrase what Ed Silvoso told our pastors in a conference, "There is not a problem with the harvest, the problem is with those harvesting. We expect the wheat to get up and walk into our barns. Someone must go out and harvest the wheat and bring it into the barn. This is what Jesus meant by 'The harvest is plenteous but the laborers are few.'"

The fact of the matter is we have plenty of church members but not enough of them are laborers in the harvest. If the pastors and leaders are unified and have a strategy for their community, the key is to mobilize church members around that strategy.

God will work with you. Mobilizing churches to pray for their communities through The Year of Answered Prayer campaign clearly drew His blessing. As a result of the campaign, the local professional baseball team, the Tampa Bay Devil Rays, called and asked if we would be interested in having an event at the Tropicana Stadium prior to a ball game. Our goal was to present Christ to the at-large Tampa Bay residents at least once a year, and God supplied the vehicle. God was supplying a big barn for a big harvest.

God gives us the venue to reach those we have been building relationships with. Raise the Roof, for instance, features the music ministry of nationally known artists, testimonies by professional athletes and a clear Gospel presentation. Each year of the first two years, more than sixteen thousand people attended, and two thousand underprivileged children were sponsored. In 2000, prior to the concert, sixty thousand pounds of food were given away to nearly six hundred needy families in a nearby park. Businesses, families, pastors, youth and compassion ministries were all mobilized to make the event a success. More than one thousand people made commitments to Christ.

The harvest is ready; will the workers come?

It is amazing that sports stadiums are being filled for evangelism. It shows what unified mobilization of God's people can accomplish. It is a testimony of God's commanded blessing to bring life forevermore to Tampa Bay. It is a testimony of what we can do together that we cannot do apart.

Another example of the impact of united mobilization comes from the former lead intercessor for German-born evangelist Reinhard Bonnke, who is known for his huge crusades in Africa.

Suzette Hattingh, intercessor turned evangelist, is mobilizing groups in European cities for city impact. Her ministry, "Voice in the City," along with local churches, is doing a new kind of city campaign called "Taking the City." Evangelist Hattingh discovered that "in Europe [the evangelistic ministries] seem to move in and out again without making a deeper impact. Europe needs a different approach [to evangelism], and I think I have found it."

Hattingh's approach is to mobilize the church to go to the city rather than expecting the city to come to the church. As she puts it, "The lost [in Europe] will not come to us." She is helping churches to become, as Steve Sjogren puts it, "A go-

and-do church rather than a come-and-see church." One tactic that is being employed is called "The Package." The Package combines various forms of evangelism: prayer, servanthood, kindness and compassion evangelism with an event where proclamation and healing take place. The church goes into the marketplace and into neighborhoods, door to door. They hand out free roses, clean homes and shop for the elderly. They give away groceries, appliances and hold a children's outreach in city parks and distribute Gospel literature. They have seen God change lives as they combine these types of evangelism with Spirit-led prayers for those they assist.

One campaign took place in Deggendorfer, Germany. Pastor Gunther Geier of Christuzentrum Ostbayern reported that the campaign resulted in 140 confirmed, immediate conversions, with many more "backslidden" believers rededicating themselves to the Lord. Geier claims that his whole church is now on fire and will keep going with an unprecedented ninety percent of the 450 members actively participating.[1]

High-Impact, Low-Maintenance Ministry

The power of one also means combining resources so that much can be done with a little. When people come to our offices, which are in a space donated by businesspeople in the community, a common question is, where is everybody? They cannot believe that, with everything that is being accomplished in the community, there are so few people in our office. It is a high-impact, low-maintenance mentality. The first-century Church did not need the buildings and budgets we need today to accomplish the work. They were unified and mobilized to glorify our resurrected Lord through "presence evangelism." His presence in a city, made visible through the actions of His people, brought in those who were lost. As we all do our part, we can accomplish much more with a lot less.

The youth are more ready than any other sector of the Church to be mobilized. They came out to the Raise the Roof event and compassion outreaches, and they made up half of the nearly fourteen hundred volunteers at the Supper Bowl event we held in Tampa.

The city of Tampa said, "Wow!" In fact it was because of the Supper Bowl that the city readily got involved in Carefest. Mayor Dick Greco of Tampa and Mayor Rick Baker of St. Petersburg sent out proclamations in support, and other local mayors have followed their lead.

It is interesting that we are working with all the same components that the Billy Graham Crusade did when it brought its mission to town. Working together during such crusades is a concept people understand. But that can unfortunately breed a mindset that the Christian community needs to work together only on special occasions. Just the opposite is true. Pulling together to reach a city for Christ ought to be the rule for the Christian community. The ongoing unity of the Christian community can be displayed or expressed through mega-events or one-time crusades, but this should be only a demonstration or an expression of what is going on continuously. I tell people that Somebody Cares is like an ongoing Billy Graham Crusade without the $3.5 million usually needed to do a crusade.

We are far from arriving. We have a long way to go. It is a continuous battle "to preserve the unity of the Spirit in the bond of peace" (Ephesians 4:3). As we press ahead to mobilize the army of God in our communities, in the faith that Christ wants to embrace our cities, the law of frequency will give us complete victory.

The Law of Frequency

Dr. Terry Teykl explains how he learned of the Law of Frequency in his book *Pray the Price*:

When I lived in College Station, home of Texas A&M University, one of my favorite places to jog was on Kyle Field, where the Aggies play football. Probably as well known as the Aggie football team is the military style marching band that is the pride of A&M.

I watched them practice many times, and was always amazed at their precision and exactness. After they finished a drill you could see a grid of circles in the Astroturf where their feet had all landed, because their steps were so carefully measured that they literally marched in each other's footprints.

One time as I was visiting with one of the drill leaders who went to my church, I commented on how impressed I was with their accuracy, and he said, "Yes, that is why when we march over a bridge, we instruct the cadets to intentionally break cadence." He explained that in physics, there is a principle known as "natural frequency," which basically says that a force on a structure that is repeated in exactly the same spot over and over, even if it is a small force, will eventually cause damage to the structure. In other words, the Aggie band could theoretically crumble a bridge just by marching on it! But the key to the force is the unity of their cadence.[2]

Since God is the author of all laws, what applies in the natural can also be applied in the spiritual. Jesus referred to it as the law of agreement in Matthew 18:19–20.

> **We will reach our cities as we respond to our leader Jesus and work together as many parts of one body, producing the *power of one*.**

How did Ehud and the Hebrews of Jericho overcome the invincible Moabite army? By faith, the many acted as one. We will reach our cities as we respond to our leader Jesus and work together as many parts of one body, producing the *power of one*.

How important to God is unity of His people doing His work? God died for it and He killed for it. Let me explain.

Ephesians 5:25 tells us Jesus died for the Church. He did not die for a harem. He died for His Bride, the Church. He bought her with His own blood. Okay, we know that. But whom did He kill for it? Ananias and Sapphira. When we read about their story in Acts 5, we can conclude that God zapped them to demonstrate that even though it was a time of grace, He is still a God of wrath and will judge sin.

A look at the history behind the story will give us another point of view. In the opening chapters of the book of Acts, we find the Holy Spirit descending on those who are in one accord, waiting obediently as Jesus had told them. In Acts we find the Church in true unity. We have already noted a good illustration of the difference between being united and having unity: You can take two cats and tie their tails together and they will be united—but there will not be much unity.

He did not die for a harem. He died for His Bride, the Church.

Unity is dominant in the first several chapters of the history of the Church. In Acts 2:1 we read that "they were all together in one place." Again in verses 44 and 46 of that same chapter we read, "And all those who had believed were *together* and had all things in common. . . . Day by day [they were] continuing with *one mind* in the temple" (emphasis added). Acts 4:24 says, "And when they heard this, they lifted their voices to God with one accord." And Acts 4:32 says, "And the congregation of those who believed were of one heart and soul; and not one of them claimed that anything belonging to him was his own, but all things were common property to them."

As a result of this unity, the Lord's embrace of the city of Jerusalem was evident. His manifest presence was prevailing in the city through His Church. Many signs and wonders took place. They shared their belongings freely so that no one would be in need, and they had favor with *all* the people (not just fellow Christians). The Lord added to their number day by day those who were being saved. The lame walked, the unsaved were saved, the average member spoke the Word of God with boldness, and people even sold their land and homes to help those in need.

The prayer of Jesus in John 17 was being fulfilled. The glory of God was manifest in the city. The Bride, Christ's Church, was experiencing the embrace of Jesus through the Holy Spirit.

Then in Acts 5 we learn that Ananias and Sapphira scheme together to make themselves look good in the eyes of the Church and at the same time hold onto their wealth. Ananias and Sapphira sell their "condo" on the river Jordan and plan to tell the Church that they are turning over all the proceeds. In reality they keep back a portion for

> **Jesus is a jealous husband. He will not tolerate sins that taint His Bride and steal His glory.**

themselves. By a supernatural word of knowledge, the apostle Peter lets them know that God, the Holy Spirit, has caught them in their greedy lie and they die instantly.

Were Ananias and Sapphira really saved or not? God is the Judge. We do know that they did not leave the Church on good terms. I believe the reason God ended their lives was because of their selfishness and greed, which led them to lie. It was a threat to the unity of God's Church. It threatened to taint His Bride, to dim the light of God's glory.

Jesus is a jealous husband. By judging the sin of Ananias and Sapphira, God was sending the message that He would not tolerate the sins of selfishness, pride and greed that taint His Bride, divide His Church and steal His glory.

In Acts 5 we see the effect of this sin being judged. "And great fear came over the whole church, and over all who heard of these things" (verse 11). Fear of the Lord manifest in a city is another way of knowing that God is present. "At the hands of the apostles many signs and wonders were taking place among the people; and they were all with *one* accord in Solomon's portico" (verse 12, emphasis added).

143

After the death of Ananias and Sapphira, everything returned to normal. Signs and wonders once again took place, the fear of the Lord was in the city and the believers were in one accord. Jesus died for the Church and I believe He killed for it to show that His manifested presence through His Church is mankind's only hope.

In my book *Praying Up a Storm*, I wrote a statement that rings truer now than before, since the murders at Columbine High School and other such incidents have taken place. "If the church is not the solution to the problems of our cities, then we will only have cities with no solution." The effort of the current presidency to turn the country toward a faith-based community is evidence that the government does not have the solution. A positive way to reword that statement is, "The Church, with Jesus Christ as the Head, is the only solution to the problems of our cities."

We Are the Only Plan God Has

Bill Anderson, a former pastor, shared this story from his childhood that illustrates the importance of unity in the Body of Christ:

God stabbed my heart about unity long before I was saved. My father was killed in an oil field accident when I was just five weeks of age. One day, as young teenagers, my sister and I were fighting. My mother came to me and it was one of the rare times in her life that I saw fear in her eyes. She is a very strong woman. She had to be. For more than sixty years now she has been without a man by her side. Raising four children by herself, she made it one day at a time, as she says, "By the grace of God."

Mother sat my sister and me down and wept as she said, "You have to get along, because you're all I have." That stabbed me. "Listen, fellow members of the Bride: There

144

are not two brides. There's only one Bride. This is the only Bride He has. If we don't do it right, nobody can."

God has no other plan. We are the plan, and that means He has confidence that Christ in us can meet the challenge. To be a mended net, we must work in unity and with a common purpose—and that purpose is to see lost souls come to Christ.

Would You?

Jesus wants to embrace your city, but before He can do that He must embrace the Bride, His Church in that city. We, His Church, can bring WOW to our cities of woe. Let it not be said of us that Jesus desired to embrace us, to bring us the WOW for our woe but that we would not.

Being a would or would-not city means that as a Church, or as a member of Christ's Church in your city, you will do certain things to welcome His embrace and experience His manifest presence. For example:

- Would you drop denominational and racial walls and come together at the cross of Christ?
- Would you prefer others above yourself?
- Would you drop your program to work together and become God's gift to your city?
- Would you turn off the TV and computer and pray?
- Would you swallow your pride and the need to be recognized?
- Would you serve another church?
- Would you reach out to those in the inner city?
- Would you drop your agenda for God's?
- Would you make unity a priority, knowing it is a mandate from Jesus?

145

- Would you stand in the gap for pastors and ministry leaders?
- Would you let God break your heart over what breaks His heart in your community?
- Would you mobilize yourself, others and your church for the Kingdom's sake in your city?
- Would you do it even though no one else does?
- Would you keep going when others give up?
- Would you do all you can to see Jesus embrace your community?

Answer these questions and others the Holy Spirit will bring to your mind not merely with words but with action. Imagine Jesus looking at your community, saying, "O (fill in your city's name), how often I want to embrace you as a hen gathers her chicks under her wings. *Will you* or *will you not* have it?"

Jesus wants you, as the big "C" Church, to be His gift to your community. Jesus wants to give your community a WOW for the present woe. He wants to inhabit the church in your community with all His fullness. He wants a harvest of souls far more than we do.

John Wesley came up with the idea "just do it" long before Nike, the athletic wear company, did. This is John Wesley's version:

Do all the good you can
By all the means you can
In all the ways you can
At all the times you can
To all the people you can
As long as ever you can.

Church, there is nothing to it but to do it! Do it and make the impact Christ intended you to have for His Kingdom.

146

13

Unifying Servant Leaders
for City Impact

The apostle Paul writes this to the church in Corinth: "For I am jealous for you with a godly jealousy; for I betrothed you to one husband, so that to Christ I might present you as a pure virgin" (2 Corinthians 11:2). Paul sees it as his responsibility to present the church in that city to Christ. Can you imagine such a roll call taking place in heaven? The Lord is sitting on His throne and the angel Gabriel declares, "Leaders from Corinth, present those in your congregations who make up Christ's Bride from your city." Paul was preparing the Bride, or Church, at Corinth to be ready to meet Jesus, the Bridegroom.

As we were beginning to bring pastors and ministries together in the Tampa Bay area, the one slogan that became a part of the initial paragraph of the covenant of unity was this: "Prepare the Bride before the Bridegroom comes." This slogan identifies our responsibility to prepare the Bride in quantity and in quality. In other words, we are to reach all those who will make up the Bride in our city with the Gospel of Jesus Christ and to bring them to a maturity in Christ. This statement also gives us a sense of urgency and hopeful expectation. The Bridegroom, Jesus Christ, is coming back for His Bride and we must be ready.

In the story of Esther, King Ahasuerus is seeking a new queen to replace the deposed Queen Vashti. He conducts a beauty pageant. Young ladies throughout the region are gathered together and put into the custody of Hegai, a eunuch. His job is to prepare these ladies, from whom the king will choose his queen.

Esther finds favor in Hegai's eyes and receives some special treatment. Hegai is a trusted friend of the king. He knows what will appeal to the king. He prepares Esther with the right cosmetics, perfume, hairstyle and dress. Esther recognizes that her own tastes and preferences are not the question. Only the king's interests matter and she submits herself completely to the suggestions of Hegai (see Esther 2:15). If you know the story, you know she found favor in the eyes of all who saw her as well as King Ahasuerus.

Today God is looking for the spiritual eunuchs who will be the leaders in their communities to make the Bride ready. Since eunuchs cannot have sexual relations, they were trusted to oversee the king's harem and the queen. Spiritually God is looking for eunuchs to lead in communities around the world—spiritual eunuchs who do not have any other desire but to serve the King. They understand that their role is to serve the Bride, making her ready for the King. They have no desire to obtain anything for themselves from the Bride. These spiritual eunuchs are trusted friends of the Bridegroom. They know His voice and as friends they do what He commands (see John 15:14). In doing so they help develop the perfect match for Jesus, a Bride without spot or wrinkle (see also 1 John 3:2–3). John the Baptist was a

148

spiritual eunuch. When asked by his disciples about Jesus, who was also baptizing, John answers:

"A man can receive nothing unless it has been given him from heaven. You yourselves are my witnesses that I said, 'I am not the Christ,' but, 'I have been sent ahead of Him.' He who has the bride is the bridegroom; but the friend of the bridegroom, who stands and hears him, rejoices greatly because of the bridegroom's voice. So this joy of mine has been made full. He must increase, but I must decrease."

John 3:27–30

He is devoted solely to one purpose and mission and that is preparing the way for the Bridegroom. He finds joy and fulfillment in his servant role, not to have the Bride, Israel, but to make her ready. Finally, he is ready to decrease at any moment. If we are to be Jesus' friends, we must become a part of the ever *decreasing* ministries that John the Baptist started.

Pastor and author Charles Swindoll recalls watching Leonard Bernstein, the famous orchestra conductor, being interviewed on television one evening. During the chat one admirer asked, "Mr. Bernstein, what is the most difficult instrument to play?" He responded with quick wit:

Second fiddle. I can get plenty of first violinists, but to find one who plays *second* violin with as much enthusiasm, or *second* French horn or *second* flute, now that's a problem. And yet if no one plays second, we have no harmony.[1]

God is looking for second-fiddle servant leaders in our communities—leaders who will decrease so that Jesus will increase. This is not just amusing; it is vital.

As we become those spiritual-eunuch leaders, we gain authority to overthrow the enemies of our cities. In 2 Kings 9:30–33 we read how Jehu has Queen Jezebel on the run.

He is hunting her down and the Bible reports what happens when he finally catches up with her:

> When Jehu came to Jezreel, Jezebel heard of it, and she painted her eyes and adorned her head and looked out the window. As Jehu entered the gate, she said, "Is it well, Zimri, your master's murderer?" Then he lifted up his face to the window and said, "Who is on my side? Who?" And two or three officials [*eunuchs*, KJV] looked down at him. He said, "Throw her down." So they threw her down, and some of her blood was sprinkled on the wall and on the horses, and he trampled her under foot.

The eunuchs were not seducible. Queen Jezebel's seductive ways had no power over them. King Ahab had authority granted to him by his position as king but never wielded his power. This is what Jezebel sought to do. The spirit of Jezebel seeks to seduce those in spiritual authority. It seeks to make them weak or lose their authority altogether by her lustful temptations.

Today, as it was in 2 Kings 9, we need leaders who are spiritual eunuchs. We need leaders who will not be seduced and who will rise up together to cast down spiritual enemies in our cities and communities. Before Jesus can embrace a city, He must embrace the church of that city. Before the church of that city is embraced, the leaders must prepare themselves and others.

Here is a summary. A spiritual-eunuch leader

- understands that his mission is to prepare others for Jesus.
- is solely devoted to that purpose.
- can be trusted.
- is Christ's friend.
- is ever decreasing so He can increase.

- is not seduced and has the spiritual authority to cast down the enemies of the Bride and Bridegroom.

As *Ehud* means "union," the first place where unity needs to take place is in leadership. In other words there will be a core of leaders among the various key groups. These are usually people who have the conviction and willingness to sacrifice to see God's purposes come about, and they are in it for the long term.

In the case of Jericho, God raised up one man to bring deliverance, *Ehud*, "union." Today God is raising up union that will act like one man to deliver the city. Even in the midst of unity among leaders, like Ehud, there will be those among leaders who are catalysts.

We can infer that Ehud, the deliverer, was raised up from among the Jews dwelling in Jericho. The leadership needed to deliver your city will also come from within your own ranks. As David Thompson, assistant to Ed Silvoso of Harvest Evangelism, has said, "The grace to reach your city is already in the city." In other words what is necessary to reach the city is already in there. The leadership is all ready but it needs to come into unity. For leaders to do that, they must become spiritual eunuchs like John the Baptist. They must go through the "Ever Decreasing School of Obedience" in order to come together humbly. Characteristics like love and humility, which make unity possible, need to start in God's ordained delegated authority. Before we can tear down the enemy from without we need to deal with the one within. In the church in America, the enemy is pride, independence and self-reliance. Those who will make unity possible will create a place of habitation for the Lord—a Bride who is irresistible to the Bridegroom's embrace.

> **Unity starts with the humble leaders who will not give in to spiritual seduction.**

If pastors will not unite and embrace the commanded blessing, where brethren dwell together in unity, God will use other parts of the Body. Whoever makes up that unity, God will bless and others will follow. As an example, Paul Yonggi Cho pastors the largest single congregation in the world with more than one million members. He realized this growth by implementing the now famous cell-church method of evangelism and discipleship. Initially he had to bypass the established leadership and recruit women who were receptive to this new concept.

Jesus reached out first to the current leadership of His day, but for the most part they rejected Him. He got His leadership from among common people. Jesus will have His Church. He will find a people who will want His embrace, and the blessings that go with it.

Psalm 133:2 states: "It [unity] is like the precious oil upon the head, coming down upon the beard, even Aaron's beard, coming down upon the edge of his robes." Unity is to start at the head and, based on this analogy from Scripture, it is to come from the priest or those with a calling from God, such as Aaron the high priest. The "precious oil" symbolizes the grace and favor that comes from the presence of the Holy Spirit. It is to run down from the head, or leadership, onto the rest of the Body.

God the Father is looking for friends of the Bridegroom, Jesus. He desires friends whom He can entrust with His Bride. He wants friends He can indwell by His Spirit, friends who will humbly serve together, preparing His Bride to receive Him. We need leaders who, as spiritual eunuchs, cannot be seduced, whose sole desire is to serve the King and make a perfect match for Him according to His desires.

Assume that there are spiritual eunuchs in your community who have humble servant hearts. It is time to find them and bring them together. How do you begin?

I will offer here a number of guidelines, but let me say first that a good starting point is to find the faithful prayer warriors in your area who have been praying for unity and who probably prayed that initiative into your heart. Ask them to pray for favor as you begin. Ask them to come and pray prior to a major event and during the pastors' meetings. Ask them for insight and to be carriers of the vision for unity in the Christian community. I have found people of prayer to be some of the most enthusiastic, long-term advocates.

1. Know That It Begins with You

It begins with one pastor, one business leader or one anointed lay person who has a heart to serve. It would be best for him or her to meet one-on-one with a few others, even a diverse few, who might make up a catalytic core. When I started I got a diverse number of pastors to lend their names to a letter. If you can get pastors of larger churches to do this, it gives credibility in some people's eyes. My experience has been that the pastors of larger churches will not usually be that involved and will not frequent your gatherings. They need to be involved, but do not expect it. Jack Hayford and Ted Haggard are exceptions, not the rule, to group involvement.

2. Meet in a Neutral, Nonthreatening Environment

In my opinion, the first meeting should be in a neutral place or in a mainline denominational church. This makes it a safe place for some who might not come otherwise. I have found those from charismatic backgrounds are much more likely to go to a conservative, mainline church than vice versa.

3. Have Only a Kingdom Agenda

The only agenda is to come together, build relationships and find God's heart to reach the community. The first year of Somebody Cares Tampa Bay, all we did was meet. By the end of the year, the Lord gave us a prayer-evangelism strategy.

4. Pray in English

Because I believe it is more important to promote unity than my worship preference or prayer style, I stress praying in English, not tongues, during our meetings. We have had some offended by this because they think we are compromising. I believe, however, that this way we can pray with fervor and passion and in a way that is edifying to everyone.

5. See Your Meeting as a Filling Station

Mark Jones, prayer pastor for City Church in Seattle, Washington, was at a prayer conference in the bay area. As he came into town, there was a news story on the radio about a fuel tanker that exploded. Though the truck was empty, the fumes left in the tank made it dangerously combustible. Mark pulled me aside at our pastors' meeting and shared an insight: "The gasoline tanker that is most likely to explode isn't the full one. It's the one that's empty. A small spark can ignite a tanker that only has fumes left. God has showed me that pastors in Tampa Bay are like that tanker. They're running on empty and are an accident waiting to happen. Daniel, you and your meetings need to be filling stations to these pastors so they can go forward with the vision of mobilizing their churches for the community. They believe in the church coming and working together, but they cannot do it because they are on empty."

> "Dan, pastors are running on empty. Your meetings need to be a filling station."

This pierced my heart because I am very task and goal oriented. I can be perceived as a rancher (someone who drives people to the place they need to go) more than a shepherd. If the people around you are on empty, any forced movement forward will be seen as driving them. Fill their tanks or you will be pushing the car up the hill.

6. Keep a Balance between Being and Doing

I have found that there are basically three types of pastors. The first is pastors who come because they just want the fellowship and prayer. The second is pastors who say, "I want to do something. I pray with my elders. I want to know what we are doing." The third type of pastor is the one somewhere in between. As a rule we should seek to minister to Christ first, through praise and worship, and then pray for one another and what we believe God wants to do in our communities.

Our groups do both. The first hour is worship and prayer for one another. We pray in small groups for individual and church needs. During the second hour, we eat a breakfast or lunch. This gives us time to eat, fellowship and then strategize or share community-wide efforts.

7. Keep Announcements to a Minimum

We provide a table where people can put flyers and announcements about upcoming events. We try to include only those things that are area-wide efforts on the agenda. Pastors hearing a bunch of announcements will be turned off quickly.

8. Establish a Core of Servant Leaders

It takes time, energy and money to bring pastors together. Pastors will need to commit some of their office staff, equipment, etc. to getting the word out. A core of pastors who want to see God's best for your community will be happy to provide these resources. A shared plurality of leadership is best so that it does not become too burdensome for any one person and no one gets burned out. Of course the best way to see pastors come together is by pastors inviting pastors. They become a sounding board to ensure success. They will help differentiate between merely good ideas and God's ideas, and will help discern God's timing.

9. Be Consistent

Given the average pastor's busy schedule, it is important to keep meetings on the same day of the week and at the same time. Having a central place to meet is generally good. But some groups may enjoy moving the meeting to each other's facilities. This is a way to get to know each other better and to pray God's blessing for the host pastor on site. Supplying lunch at one's building is a good way to promote unity of the Body. We have pastors choose a specific month to host so we can schedule at least six months in advance.

10. Consider a Paid or Subsidized Administrator

In larger cities maintaining databases is an ongoing process. There is a great deal of turnover in the ministry, so this is a hard area to maintain.

11. Keep the Vision

With so many activities pulling at them, it is easy for pastors to shove these meetings and unity efforts to the side. They will need constant reminders, scripturally and practically, to keep the momentum going. Be in it for the long haul. Keep alive a picture of faith, hope and perseverance that is necessary to receive God's blessing.

12. Build Biblical Convictions for Unity

When Buck Jacobs, founder of C12, writes to businesspeople, he mentions that "Priorities are what we do; everything else is just talk." Scriptures on unity are not the ones most pastors are diving into daily. They are focusing more on feeding their flocks. It is good to go over passages that remind them of God's priority. We must bring out the Scriptures and believe God will cause the convictions to be acted upon so that efforts to unify become a priority. Share accomplishments that have taken place that would not have otherwise. Allow testimonies to take place on how they have been blessed by coming and doing things together.

13. Have Pastors Choose Points of Contact

We do a number of things annually through the Somebody Cares network, from forty days of prayer to Carefest week with activities in between. At first glance this can appear overwhelming to a pastor. Pastors do not want more to do, but they do want their people mobilized effectively to have an impact on the community. Choosing or delegating individuals to help with a city-wide prayer effort or a back-to-school campaign is a way to get members involved without overwhelming the pastor. What we do is create avenues for people to become laborers in something bigger than themselves. With people appointed to carry out the various community projects and efforts, the people become laborers. The pastor just needs to promote it from the pulpit.

14. Beware of the Consumer Mentality

Pastors are aware of this mindset because they get it from their people. It says, "I tithe or put a certain amount of money into the offering. I expect, therefore, to have such and such program, etc." A consumer mentality says, "It is all about me, my wants and my needs."

Pastors can have that mentality as well. They might say, "If I agree to be part of that effort, I need to see immediate results—like people coming to my church." We find out later that it just did not work for them, and they drop out.

I believe that we need to be good stewards and that our efforts will eventually bear results. God the Holy Spirit is the author of the results. We need to understand that we are planting seeds of revival. Everything may not have an immediate return. We need to have other barometers and ask such questions as: How did it change the atmosphere in our city? Or even among our churches? What kind of testimony was it to our cities, civic and business leaders? What happened in the hearts of my people for having been involved?

15. Emphasize the Benefits, How God Has Blessed

We are usually in the media spotlight several times a year, through television and the local newspapers. One particular day, on the front page of the metro section, was a story about our unified outreach to the city. Also on the metro front page that day was a story about a local pastor who was getting a divorce and whose wife wanted money from the sale of their church building. At first we wondered, "Why did that have to run on the same day?" On second thought, we began to praise God because, without our collective outreach, that would have been the only testimony about the Church to the community that day.

The benefits can be measured in souls saved, people mobilized, resources shared and money being used more wisely. We are able to do more with what we have. By working together, our dollars for outreach are sometimes doubled or tripled. This is the case in our back-to-school program. Because we work together, churches are now getting three or four backpacks to distribute for what they used to pay for one. And as we noted earlier, because of our cooperation, stadium venues have opened up and local church committees are now doing their own back-to-school outreaches. This is just one of many examples I could give.

You never know when a seed will bear fruit. Jim Tarr, pastor of Immanuel Chapel in Largo, Florida, helped distribute forty thousand New Testaments. Several months later six people visited his church and gave their lives to Christ. When Pastor Tarr asked them how they heard about this church, they responded, "Your members put New Testaments on our doors, encouraging us to read about Jesus. We have been reading faithfully and decided it was time to visit your church."

16. Create a Place Where Leaders Can Be Vulnerable

Being a pastor is one of the most demanding, stressful occupations there is. Pastors need to share their struggles with others who understand and can bring insight or encouragement. If the pastor is not healthy, most likely the church will not be either. Len Harper, pastor of South Brandon Worship Center in Brandon, Florida, shares this:

> I decided to test these pastors and see if they were competitive or if they had hearts for others and were Kingdom men.

Shortly before I began pastoring the South Brandon Worship Center, a pastor friend invited me to attend a Somebody Cares pastors' meeting, saying that I would be encouraged. This church was a new challenge for me. My other pastorates experienced immediate success. This church continued to decline, with the worship leader taking a group and starting another work.

I decided to test these pastors and see if they were competitive or if they had hearts for others and were Kingdom men. I opened up and became vulnerable, sharing how difficult the church was and how depressed I had become. The pastors gathered around me and prayed. I sensed an immediate release but more importantly I knew they cared about Len Harper as a person not only as a pastor. They spoke encouragement into my life. From there, my friendship has deepened with these men. My church has also turned the corner and has doubled in size. There is unity among the members and we are able to join with others to bless the community. Now I am able to be there for other pastors and bring healing and encouragement to them.

17. Take Time to Hang Out

One way to create an atmosphere that allows pastors to be vulnerable is by becoming friends. Pastor Mike Modica of First Assembly in Deland, Florida, has headed the pastors' meetings there for more than a decade. He says they have learned to hang out together. They go fishing, golfing and to ball games. They take trips together, go on double dates with their spouses and become real friends.

18. Unity Is Not Always Convenient

Fostering unity will take sacrifice but it will be worth it. When Solomon dedicated the Temple (see 1 Kings 8), the leaders brought their sacrifices. They sacrificed 120,000 sheep and 22,000 oxen. With these sacrifices, the glory of the Lord filled the Temple. If we desire to see the glory of the Lord in our communities, we need to offer up our schedules and become available for what God wants. As leaders we must yield the need for notoriety, our programs and agendas. We need to release our people to pursue what God wants to do to benefit the whole Body, have an impact on the city and enlarge God's Kingdom.

19. Dig In for the Long Haul

The community transformations some of you may have heard about all took place over long periods of time. This shows that our commitment must be long-term. The following testimonial from Victoria, Australia, sent to me from Pastor Anthony Townsend, on behalf of the Bellarine Pastors' Network, supports this idea.

The Bellarine Peninsula is located in Victoria, Australia, and is an area made up of a number of small and larger towns with a population of around forty thousand people. In 1996 I felt a call from God to bring pastors together with the aim to establish and build meaningful relationships among them. I learned that true spiritual unity can never be based on events, doctrine or tradition. Rather it needs to be based on heart-to-heart relationships through the love of Christ. This leads to trust being built, which, in turn, leads to working more effectively together to have an impact on the community with the Gospel of Jesus Christ.

As a group of pastors, we meet to pray for one another and for our region. We have lunch together every six weeks, which includes a time of encouragement, prayer and fellowship. We have a network of eleven churches with nineteen ministers committed to building relationships.

After seven years of building relationships, you realize that it takes long-term commitment, perseverance and being very intentional about it. It does not happen overnight. You have to be in for the long haul and committed to serving your co-workers in Christ and the community. The practical outworking of our unity has resulted in strong working relationships among pastors in doing outreaches.

We do several outreaches together. One is a youth outreach to the middle schools. We go into the schools weekly with activities and short devotionals. Another project is connecting with our community leaders. We visit them and pray for them. We offer support and encouragement.

We believe God is preparing the ground for a significant move of His Spirit. As a minister related it, revival is digging a hole in the desert while confidently believing God will send the rain to fill it. We are continuing to dig deep with a strong expectation that God will pour out His Spirit to bring transformation to this region.

20. The Body Must Be Formed Before God Breathes Life

God formed Adam and then breathed life into him. The Body of Christ was formed in the Upper Room and God

161

breathed on them. The point is that God breathes His life into bodies already formed. As leaders we need to be committed to forming a unified Body so the Holy Spirit will breathe His manifest power and presence into our cities through us.

21. Recognize That They Cannot Always Be Involved

Churches, for a variety of reasons, cannot be involved with everything, even *big* things. They choose what strikes them and ignites their passion. Show that you want to help facilitate what they are already doing rather than tug on them to do another activity.

22. Emphasize That God Blesses Obedience

Most of our cities are in the condition they are because of our disobedience as His Church. Our obedience is necessary to change our communities morally. We do it because it is right, whether the results are manifested or not. If we continue to operate with the same old mentality, then we will continue to lose ground to Satan in our cities. We need to obey God. Obeying Christ's prayer to be one is the path for the Church from now until He returns. Failing to do so exposes us to woe. Even worse, we miss out on bringing God's WOW. By cooperating with others we become God's gift and instrument to save thousands in our cities.

23. Participate in Monthly Conference Calls

On the second Tuesday of every month I host a teleconference (a conference by phone) that allows city leaders from across the continent to explore a topic with featured guests and then interact during a question-and-answer period. Mission America provides this forum so we can be informed and encouraged by the experiences of others who are like-minded. Another such teleconference takes place the third Thursday of each month. To learn how to participate in these calls or start one for your region, email info@cityreaching.com.

24. Attend a Roundtable or Conference

Each winter Somebody Cares, Tampa Bay hosts a hands-on City Impact conference that covers prayer, compassion, creative evangelism, unity, marketplace ministry and more. The Mission America Coalition provides City Impact Roundtables (CIR), peer-to-peer meetings of Christian leaders who are prayerfully seeking the unity of the Church for holistic evangelism and the revival and renewal of the Church, leading to cultural awakening and transformation. The Mission America coalition comprises leaders from more than eighty denominations, three hundred servant ministry organizations and fifty ministry networks, each sharing the vision of bringing together "the whole Church to pray over and discuss how to collaborate in taking the whole Gospel to the whole City." See the contact information on the last page of the book.

25. Be Kingdom Driven

Coming together is a means to an end. Our purpose in doing so is not merely for unity's sake, but to have a greater impact on our communities, thus establishing the Lord's Kingdom. The video *Quickening*, released by George Otis Jr. and the Sentinel Group, defines succinctly what it means to be a servant leader who is Kingdom driven: "Servant leaders count the cost, stay the course and direct people to a Kingdom not their own."
Amen?

Afterword

The great revivalist Charles Finney once said, "Revival is no more a miracle than a crop of wheat." We know that when a grain of wheat falls into the ground and dies, it will produce a harvest (see John 12:24). Daniel, in this book, has helped to articulate some key principles of dying to ourselves, while having an impact on our communities in very tangible ways. It not only takes inspiration and revelation from the Lord to have an impact on our communities, but a willingness to labor in the harvest together—willingness to become part of something bigger than ourselves. While men reach for thrones to build their own kingdoms, Jesus reached for a towel to wash men's feet. I have seen how many have initially become very excited about the possibilities of community impact and revival only to wane in their inspiration after the romance stage passes.

City reaching and community transformation have been frequent topics of discussion in recent years. As the founder of "Somebody Cares America/International," I have been in cities around the nation and globe, and have seen many great initiatives and community processes begun. I have also seen how some never seem to get beyond the initial stages and eventually fizzle. I like what Pastor Ron Johnson at Bethel Temple in Norfolk, Virginia, shared with me once. He said, "It seems that what starts as a great idea for prayer and unity eventually turns into a time of 'navel-gazing' sessions." I have come to the conclusion that passion without purpose will eventually wane. Without a vision (focus) and purpose of destination, all of our good intentions will be just that.

What I appreciate about Daniel and this book is that it is not written out of the ivory tower of theory but from the crucible of experience. He has a valid word to help bless our cities that comes out of personal and corporate life experiences. Through prayer, compassion and evangelism initiatives, themes found throughout the pages of this book, you have found helpful tools and ideas for your own community. As you have seen, Daniel is a strategic practitioner, embracing his own city in very tangible ways and helping others to do the same. My prayer is that you will be in that number of practitioners in reaching your community.

The opportunities for effective ministry have never been greater. It is my privilege to serve George Otis Jr. as a member of his board of directors on the Sentinel group (producers of the *Transformation* documentaries). Just a few short years ago, there were only eight communities around the world where significant transformation was clearly taking place. Today, there are more than 175 communities experiencing significant and tangible moves of God. There seem to be some key commonalities in each city, community or even nation whereby it becomes fertile and conditioned soil for the Holy Spirit. Unity of the Body is critical. Unity is not necessarily the goal, but it becomes the means to attain something greater. I have quoted Daniel Bernard numerous times, as well as in my book *Somebody Cares*, when he says, "Whereas you can tie the tails of two cats together, you may make them united but they are not in unity." So

166

true. Our meetings do not produce any synergistic impact in our communities but serving together does.

Through this book, may you be aptly motivated and convicted. Convictions not acted upon end up in a graveyard called "good intentions." Good intentions are not good enough. I implore you to unify your community and invite God's presence. It is through that place of intimacy that the Body can corporately join hands and hearts to share the love of Christ. Embrace your city and gain a better understanding of how to reach out to your city in a tangible expression of Christ's love. We can truly become a mended net, cast into the sea of souls, fulfilling the Great Commission together.

Doug Stringer

Twenty-seven Reasons Why the Church Needs the Poor

1. To remind us that we are "poor in spirit" (Matthew 5:3).
2. To keep us humble and recipients of His grace. "God is opposed to the proud, but gives grace to the humble" (James 4:6).
3. To emulate the work of Jesus on earth. Disciples sent by John the Baptist asked Jesus if He was the Messiah or should they look for another. Jesus responded by saying, "The blind receive sight, the lame walk, the lepers are cleansed, and the deaf hear, the dead are raised up, the poor have the gospel preached to them" (Luke 7:22).
4. To honor God. Proverbs 14:31 says, "He who oppresses the poor taunts his Maker, but he who is gracious to the needy honors Him."
5. To be happy. Proverbs 14:21 says, "He who despises his neighbor sins, but happy is he who is gracious to the poor."
6. To avoid being judged. Ezekiel 34:2–4 says, "Thus says the Lord GOD, 'Woe, shepherds of Israel who have been feeding themselves! . . . Those who are sickly you have not strengthened, the diseased you have not healed, the broken you have not bound

up, the scattered you have not brought back, nor have you sought for the lost.'"

7. To minister to Jesus and be welcomed into His Kingdom. Read Matthew 25:31–46 about the parable of the sheep and goats.

8. To be a New Testament church. New Testament churches structured their leadership to deal with the widowed and needy (see Acts 2:44–47; 6:1–7).

9. To have pure religion (see James 1:27).

10. To know God. In Jeremiah 22:16, the Lord speaks through the prophet to admonish the current king of Judah to be like King Josiah before him: "'He pled the cause of the afflicted and needy; then it was well. Is not that what it means to know Me,' declares the LORD."

11. So as not to become like Sodom. Ezekiel 16:49 says, "Behold, this was the guilt of your sister Sodom: she and her daughters had arrogance, abundant food and careless ease, but she did not help the poor and needy."

12. To show forth fruit of true repentance. Luke 3:11 says, "[John the Baptist] would answer and say to them, 'The man who has two tunics is to share with him who has none; and he who has food is to do likewise.'"

13. To get your wedding garments ready for the marriage supper of the Lamb (see Revelation 19:7–8).

14. So as not to be a respecter of persons (see James 2).

15. So we can shine in darkness (see Isaiah 58:10).

16. To have the assurance of our prayers being answered (see Isaiah 58:9).

17. To be blessed with supernatural guidance from God (see Isaiah 58:11).

18. So we will receive divine protection. Isaiah 58:8 says, "Your righteousness will go before you; the glory of the LORD will be your rear guard."

19. To fulfill God's chosen fast (see Isaiah 58:6–7).

20. To have favor and a righteous name that precedes you (see Isaiah 58:8).

21. To get a breakthrough (see Isaiah 58:8).

22. To fulfill your calling as the restorer of broken lives, broken relationships and broken cities (see Isaiah 58:12).

23. To be welcomed by Jesus to inherit the Kingdom (see Matthew 25:34).

24. To experience quick healing (see Psalm 41:3; Isaiah 58:8).

25. To be called blessed on the earth (see Psalm 41:1–2).

26. To be blessed in your work and in all your undertakings (see Deuteronomy 15:7–10).

27. To define ourselves as true followers of Christ. When John the Baptist looks for a confirmation that Jesus is the Messiah, Jesus responds by saying, "The good news is preached to the poor" (see Matthew 11:5). Ministering to the poor identifies Jesus as the Messiah. This should define us as His followers.

Town of Inglis Proclamation

135 Highway 40 West
Post Office Drawer 429
Inglis, Florida 34449

(352) 447-2203
(352) 447-2204
Fax (352) 447-1879

PROCLAMATION

Be it known from this day forward that Satan, ruler of darkness, giver of evil, destroyer of what is good and just, is not now, nor ever again will be, a part of this town of Inglis. Satan is hereby declared powerless, no longer ruling over, nor influencing, our citizens.

In the past, Satan has caused division, animosity, hate, confusion, ungodly acts on our youth, and discord amoung our friends and loved ones. NO LONGER!

The body of Jesus Christ, those citizens cleansed by the Blood of the Lamb, hereby join together to bind the forces of evil in the Holy Name of Jesus. We have taken our town back for the Kingdom of God. We are taking everything back that the devil ever stole from us. We will never again be deceived by satanic and demonic forces.

As blood-bought children of God, we exercise our authority over the devil in Jesus' name. By that authority, and through His Blessed Name, we command all satanic and demonic forces to cease their activities and depart the town of Inglis.

As the Mayor of Inglis, duly elected by the citizens of this town, and appointed by God to this position of leadership, I proclaim victory over Satan, freedom for our citizens, and liberty to worship our Creator and Heavenly Father, the God of Israel. I take this action in accordance with the words of our Lord and Savior, Jesus Christ, as recorded in Matthew 28:18-20 and Mark 16:15-18.

Signed and seal this 5th day of November, 2001.

CAROLYN RISHER, MAYOR

SALLY McCRANIE, TOWN CLERK

Notes

Chapter One: God's Gift to Your City

1. Steve Sjogren, *The Perfectly Imperfect Church: Redefining the "Ideal" Church* (Loveland, Colo.: Flagship Church Resources from Group Publishing, 2002), 147.

2. Ibid., 148–50.

3. Adapted from Don Maddox, "Our Lord's Community Church," in a September 1987 church bulletin from the First Presbyterian Church of Corona, California.

Chapter Five: Giving Birth to God's Grace for Your City

1. Jack Hayford, *Loving Your City into the Kingdom* (Ventura, Calif.: Regal Books, 1997), 14.

2. George Otis Jr., *Transformations II*, Sentinel Group, 2001.

Chapter Six: Unity Is Our Deliverer

1. Quoted in Tommy Tenney, *The God Chasers* (Shippensburg, Pa.: Destiny Image Publishers), 53.

2. Terry Teykl, *Pray the Price United Methodist: United in Prayer* (Muncie, Ind.: Prayer Point Press, 1997), 148.

Chapter Eight: A Message from God for the Devil

1. Teykl, *Pray the Price United Methodist*, 148.

173

Chapter Ten: Marketplace Impact

1. Buck Jacobs, "Working 'On' My Ministry in God's Business: Your Business as a Vehicle for Ministry" (Atlanta, Ga.: C12 Group, 2003).

Chapter Eleven: Compassion—the Key to City Impact

1. Bill Phillips, *Body for Life* (New York: Harper Collins, 1999), 34.

Chapter Twelve: The Power of One

1. Tomas Dixon, "She Dared to Claim a Continent," *Charisma* (October 2002): 65.
2. Teykl, *Pray the Price United Methodist*, 34.

Chapter Thirteen: Unifying Servant Leaders for City Impact

1. Charles R. Swindoll, *Improving Your Serve* (Waco, Tex.: Word Books, 1981), 118.

Daniel G. Bernard, who attended Kentucky Christian College, Cincinnati Bible Seminary and Liberty Theological Seminary, met and married his wife, Kathy, while working on his master's degree. They have been married for twenty years and have six children: Leah, Luke, Bethany, Faith, Peter, and Rachel.

He and Kathy pastored churches in Williamstown, Kentucky, and Bryan, Texas, where they started Full House Ministries, Inc., leading street ministry and short-term mission trips to Nigeria and Mexico. In January 1991 the Bernards left the United States to plant churches and develop a discipleship school in Nigeria. The work continues there with nine established churches.

In December 1996 Daniel and Kathy helped establish Somebody Cares, Tampa Bay (now an affiliate of Somebody Cares, America) in order to unify and mobilize churches across denominational and racial lines, utilizing all the key components needed to reach the Tampa Bay area for Jesus Christ. Through many projects and events, Somebody Cares, Tampa Bay, equips and supplies churches with resources to significantly increase their effectiveness in evangelizing the Bay area.

Under Daniel's direction, Somebody Cares has established seven monthly pastors' meetings, helped forge a "Covenant of Unity," led "The Year of Answered Prayer" and assisted with a Billy Graham Crusade. It has become the local outreach center for Operation Blessing, distributing more than 1,300,000 pounds of food annually. It also oversaw the distribution of more than a half-million "Books of Hope" in the Tampa Bay area and 15,000 backpacks through a "Back-to-School" giveaway.

Somebody Cares has been active in putting on events like "Raise the Roof," an evangelistic concert that draws over 15,000, and "Supper Bowl 2001" prior to Super Bowl XXXV, a one-day event reaching out to the community with food, clothing, and health and educational provisions.

Between 10,000–12,000 attended that event with more than 1,400 volunteers, yielding 1,210 decisions for Christ.

In September 2000 Daniel was awarded an honorary doctorate in theology from Tabernacle Bible College and Seminary in Tampa, Florida.

To be in touch with Daniel Bernard, contact:

Somebody Cares, Tampa Bay
P.O. Box 4486
Clearwater, FL 33758
1-888-561-2273
united4him@sctb.org
www.sctb.org

The City Impact movement in the United States is shepherded by the Mission America Coalition's City/Community Ministries team. If you would like to learn from others working in cities across the continent, you can be connected—via monthly nationwide conference calls, the City Impact Roundtable and a website—with believers with a similar passion and calling. Contact:

Mission America Coalition
7340 Hunters Run
Eden Prairie, MN 55346
(952) 975-0516
info@cityreaching.com
www.CityReaching.com
www.MissionAmerica.org